Learning
Interventions
for Consultants

Fundamentals of Consulting Psychology Book Series

APA FUNDAMENTALS OF CONSULTING PSYCHOLOGY

Learning Interventions for Consultants

BUILDING THE TALENT THAT DRIVES BUSINESS

MANUEL LONDON AND THOMAS DIAMANTE

AMERICAN PSYCHOLOGICAL ASSOCIATION
Washington, DC

Published by
American Psychological Association
750 First Street, NE
Washington, DC 20002
www.apa.org

APA Order Department
P.O. Box 92984
Washington, DC 20090-2984
Phone: (800) 374-2721; Direct: (202) 336-5510
Fax: (202) 336-5502; TDD/TTY: (202) 336-6123
Online: http://www.apa.org/pubs/books
E-mail: order@apa.org

In the U.K., Europe, Africa, and the Middle East, copies may be ordered from
Eurospan Group
c/o Turpin Distribution
Pegasus Drive
Stratton Business Park
Biggleswade, Bedfordshire
SG18 8TQ United Kingdom
Phone: +44 (0) 1767 604972
Fax: +44 (0) 1767 601640
Online: https://www.eurospanbookstore.com/apa
E-mail: eurospan@turpin-distribution.com

Typeset in Minion by Circle Graphics, Inc., Columbia, MD

Printer: Edwards Brothers Malloy, Lillington, NC
Cover Designer: Naylor Design, Washington, DC

Library of Congress Cataloging-in-Publication Data
Names: London, Manuel, author. | Diamante, Thomas, author.
Title: Learning interventions for consultants : building the talent that
   drives business / Manuel London and Thomas Diamante.
Description: Washington, DC : American Psychological Association, [2018] |
   Includes bibliographical references and index.
Identifiers: LCCN 2018003619| ISBN 9781433829253 | ISBN 1433829258
Subjects: LCSH: Organizational learning. | Employee training. | Business
   consultants. | Personnel management.
Classification: LCC HD58.82 .L66 2018 | DDC 658.3/124—dc23 LC record available at
https://lccn.loc.gov/2018003619

British Library Cataloguing-in-Publication Data
A CIP record is available from the British Library.

Printed in the United States of America
First Edition

http://dx.doi.org/10.1037/0000094-000

10 9 8 7 6 5 4 3 2 1

Contents

Series Editor's Foreword

Rodney L. Lowman

The field of consulting psychology has blossomed in recent years. It covers the application of psychology in consultation to organizations and systems, as well as at the individual and team levels. Unfortunately, there are very few graduate training programs in this field of specialization, so consulting psychology roles are mostly populated by those who entered the field after having trained in other areas of psychology—including industrial–organizational (I/O), clinical/counseling, and school psychology, among others. Yet such training is rarely focused on consulting psychology and psychologists, and graduate students have to learn through on-the-job training, reading books and articles, attending conferences and workshops, and being mentored in the foundational competencies of the field as they seek to transition into it.

After a number of years of editing *Consulting Psychology Journal: Practice and Research*, the field's flagship journal, I felt that an additional type of educational product was needed to help those transitioning into consulting psychology. The Society of Consulting Psychology therefore partnered with the American Psychological Association to create a new book series. The idea was to create a series of monographs on specific fundamental skill sets needed to practice in this area of specialization. Working with an Advisory Board (initially consisting of Drs. Judith Blanton, Dale Fuqua, Skipton Leonard, Edward Pavur, Jr., and myself), our goal in this book series has been to identify the major competencies needed by consulting psychologists and then to work with qualified authors to create short, accessible but evidence-based texts that would be useful both as stand-alone volumes and in combination with one another. The readers would be graduate students in relevant training programs, psychologists planning a transition into consulting psychology, and practicing professionals who want to add to their areas of expertise.

What constitutes fundamental skills in consulting psychology? The educational guidelines created by the Society of Consulting Psychology and approved by the American Psychological Association (2007), and my own *An Introduction to Consulting Psychology: Working With Individuals, Groups, and Organizations* (Lowman, 2016) and *Handbook of Organizational Consulting Psychology* (Lowman, 2002), provide useful starting points. Both of these contributions were organized around the concept of levels (individual, group, and organizational) as a taxonomy for identifying fundamental skills. Within those categories, two broad skill sets are needed: assessment and intervention.

As with many areas of psychological practice, the foundational skills that apply in one area may overlap into others in the taxonomy. Interventions with individuals, as in executive coaching, for instance, usually take place in the context of the focal client's work with a specific team and within a specific organization, which itself may also constitute a client. Understanding the system-wide issues and dynamics at the organizational level usually also involves work with specific executives and teams. And multicultural/international issues suffuse all of our roles. The APA Guidelines and the *Handbook* concluded, properly, that consulting psychologists need to be trained in and have at least foundational skills and experience at the individual, group, and organizational levels, even if they primarily specialize in one of these areas.

In inviting you to learn more about consulting psychology through this book series, I hope you will come to agree that there is no more exciting or inherently interesting area of study today than consulting psychology. The series aims not just to cover relevant literature on timeless topics in consulting psychology but also to capture the richness of this work by including case material that illustrates its applications. Readers will soon understand that consulting psychologists are real-world activists, unafraid to work in real-world environments.

Finally, as one who trained in both I/O and clinical psychology, I should note that consulting psychology has been the one area in which I felt that all of my training and skill sets were both welcome and needed. And in a world where organizations and the individuals and teams within them greatly need help in functioning effectively, in bridging individual, group, and organization-level needs and constituencies, and in coping with the rapid expansion of knowledge and escalating competition and internationalization, this book series aims to make a difference by helping more psychologists join the ranks of qualified consulting psychologists. Collectively, we can influence not just an area of specialization in psychology, but also the world.

ABOUT THIS BOOK

Learning Interventions for Consultants: Building the Talent That Drives Business is an important and timely contribution to the Fundamentals of Consulting Psychology series. As the pace of new knowledge and of organizational change continuously accelerates, consultants must grapple with how to help organizations and the groups and the individuals within them effectively learn. Indeed, whatever the focus of an intervention or assessment, learning is never far. Wise consultants learn the fundamentals and apply them in a range of consulting applications.

Both authors—Manuel London and Thomas Diamante—have had diverse careers applying psychological knowledge in corporate and other organizational worlds, and helping to extend applied knowledge. As a widely published academic (e.g., London, 2011; Sessa & London, 2006) and a senior academic administrator, Dr. London has had remarkably broad experience addressing a number of important topics in organizational psychology. Dr. Diamante, also an industrial–organizational psychologist by training, has devoted much of his professional career to organizational consulting. His professional practice has focused, among other areas, on change management and learning facilitation.

These authors' respective areas of expertise have been artfully used to create a practical and applied, yet literature-anchored, volume on the essentials of learning and training applications in consultation. The book is both pragmatic and sophisticated in its approach and will be of use to new and experienced consultants alike.

Learning Interventions for Consultants

Introduction

E mployee development is a driver of economic growth. Employees and organizations are part of what the Danish economist B. A. Lundvall called the *learning economy*, in which knowledge is the critical resource and the most important process is learning (Lundvall & Johnson, 1994). Learning is the currency that drives innovation. In an era of constant change, globalization, and emerging technologies, the necessity for innovation is indisputable. Examples of new thinking, new learning, and new outcomes appear along with robotics, coding, big data, artificial intelligence, and "the Internet of things," to name a few technologies. Cyberplatforms encourage collaborative learning and problem solving. These innovations are occurring in an increasingly tight economic climate. Business and nonprofit organizations are aware of the uncertainty of markets and the emergence of new, better, cheaper and faster methods

http://dx.doi.org/10.1037/0000094-001
Learning Interventions for Consultants: Building the Talent That Drives Business, by M. London and T. Diamante

of production, distribution, and communication. Organizations expect to hire people with the technical skills and knowledge they need at the moment. They also expect them to have basic skills, including communications, critical thinking, empathy, ethical leadership, cross-cultural sensitivity, collaboration, teamwork, and more generally speaking, emotional intelligence (Capelli, 1999).

Today's organizations also expect employees to be continuous learners, to maintain and increase their skills and competencies to keep up with the rapid pace of change and competition. Melanie Kirk, senior vice president of human resources (HR) for FreshDirect, a fast-growing online grocer, stated that companies should develop employees with as many skillsets as possible (FEDCAP Solution Series, 2016). This includes *readiness* for training—the desire and ability to learn. Learning to learn becomes a critical skill that people acquire through the experience of learning and receiving positive reinforcement for using what they learn. Employees need to realize that ongoing learning is essential for their own career stability and growth. Those who do not realize this are at risk. Employees need to take responsibility for their own career development by understanding the skills and knowledge required in the organization and by being open to learning to meet current needs and prepare for the future (London, 1996; Tannous, 2016). The organization's role in support of employee learning is to provide the enabling resources.

This book guides learning consultants in how to design, implement, and support employee development programs. The consultant's role is to provide empirically based professional assistance in the design and implementation of policies, strategies, and programs for employee development. Learning consultants may be trained psychologists and educators, or they may be managers who have functional and/or technical experience in the organization as subject matter experts. They may work with HR managers to develop performance management systems that include selection, training, performance appraisal, feedback, and career development. In a market flooded by self-proclaimed solutions of all kinds, we guide consultants as learning professionals in theory and research-based approaches in order to direct them toward what works and what does not. Training consultants assess learning needs, identifying the skills and knowledge needed by the organization today and in the foreseeable future, the extent to which employees have these skills and knowledge, and what they need to learn to close the gap and prepare for the future.

A few words about terminology: We often use the term *learning* instead of *training*, with a focus on the learner and the role of the consultant as the facilitator of learning. The term *training* suggests specific, formal learning events focused on a technical body of knowledge. *Learning* signifies a broader concept that encompasses a wide range of goals, methods, and assessments. Learning may be self-directed and experiential. It can also be vicarious (by watching others). It occurs on the job and in structured programs. It may be achieved through one or more technologies (e.g., mobile apps), and a variety of experiences such as assessments, role-plays, and games or business simulations. Training, in the narrower sense of structured education, is still important—therefore, we discuss it as part of the learning process throughout the book—but there is much more to learning, given the impact of technology and the diversity and complexity of work experiences. The accelerated pace of information dissemination and of social and organizational change creates challenges for learning professionals.

The term *development*, often conjoined with *learning*, is broader still. It refers to ongoing employee growth that prepares employees for the future in their current job or in jobs to come. The employee's goal may be career advancement—that is, to attain increasing levels of responsibility, challenge, and compensation. The organization's goal is to retain and enhance talent in order to sustain and strengthen the organization. Development is a process, not an event. It is the ongoing activation of a capability to learn, adapt, and grow. It implies experiences that contribute to employees' general abilities and value to the organization. Supervisors and managers at higher levels of the organization may be coaches and mentors who help employees understand their strengths and weaknesses, recognize opportunities for advancement in the organization, and understand the needs of the organization today and in the future.

Individual learning is acquiring knowledge and skills that are needed now or in the near future to perform work (i.e., training) and building capacity over time to assume increasing responsibility (i.e., development). *Team learning* involves team members learning about each other and how to interact to meet changing conditions. *Organizational learning* enhances the readiness of the organization as a unit to work effectively and, when needed, change goals, policies, and programs.

We distinguish between three learning processes: adaptive, generative, and transformative learning. *Adaptive learning* is about incrementally building skills and knowledge using the more traditional training method of a teacher passing down information to a student. *Generative learning* is more focused on learners figuring out how to apply skills and knowledge themselves, integrating knowledge and experiences to arrive at new ways of working. *Transformative learning* is frame breaking—for instance, shifting to a behavioral style that supports a transition to a new business strategy, leading others using new tactics to underscore the reinforcement of new competencies (i.e., talent development), changing one's assumptions about how to enhance workforce motivation, and questioning what and how one operates personally toward achievement of new goals (Mezirow, 2000).

Building on theory, research, and practice in the psychology of learning, HR development, and organization change, we articulate a five-step process for learning design and delivery:

1. assessing needs of individuals, teams, and organizations—similar to an initial clinical intake, identifying needs and considering when and how the client may benefit before proceeding;
2. contracting with clients—setting learning objectives in relation to the broader goals of the organization, conducting more in-depth needs analyses, and establishing a contract for Steps 3 through 5;
3. designing and beta testing learning methods;
4. implementing the learning intervention(s); and
5. evaluating the interventions for continuous improvement.

These steps may repeat over time, possibly in a cycle, for instance, where the evaluation becomes the needs analysis for further learning. Also, we discuss opportunities to use social media and other electronic and mobile technologies for learning, offering case examples and recommendations for application.

This book is for consulting psychologists and those new to consultative roles. We also intend the book to appeal to nonpsychologists, such as learning consultants, corporate-based facilitators of learning, and others who are interested in specific aspects of training and development, such as instructional design, learning efficacy, and/or experimentation with emerging technologies.

Throughout this book, we use the terms *consulting psychologist, learning professional, training professional, facilitator of learning,* and *consultant* interchangeably. We use the term *client* generically, whether the learning is aimed at the organization, team, or individual. The client may be the organization as a whole or one or more teams within an organization. Of course, consultants work with individuals. This could be the CEO, another "C" level executive (e.g., chief talent, learning, or training officer), a team leader, team members, or subject matter experts. These clients may act on behalf of themselves to increase their own learning, that of their unit, or the entire organization.

In Chapter 1, we describe the perspectives that consultants bring to learning interventions. They can design, deliver, and evaluate learning in the corporate classroom, online, and on the job. In Chapter 2, we focus on the science of learning, examining seminal theory and research that show the value of learning interventions to individuals, teams, and organizations. Chapter 3 describes five steps for creating training design and implementation: needs analysis, contracting, design, implementation, and evaluation. Chapter 4 focuses on the practice of learning, describing learning interventions for adaptive, generative, and transformative learning. We cover learning that helps people adapt their behaviors as they acquire competencies that are immediately applicable for improved job performance and for longer-term transformational change. Chapter 5 covers integrating technology into learning interventions, for instance, examples of blended approaches for in-person and self-paced e-learning. Finally, Chapter 6 offers recommendations for learning professionals, the challenges they face, and directions for the future.

We offer examples throughout the text, and each chapter includes one or more cases. These examples and cases exemplify the importance of needs analyses. In addition, they show how evaluations can improve learning methods and outcomes. The cases highlight the limitations of real-world practice, for instance, that learning design and implementation are constrained by resources, timelines, leaders' goals, and organizational culture. They also show that learning interventions are part of, and contribute to, broader organizational initiatives. As such, learning professionals are not merely service providers but also facilitators of organizational change.

1

The Consultant
as a Learning Professional

When it comes to leadership, the most successful companies do not recruit leaders, they develop them, and development is the key to retaining top leadership talent (Thomson, 2016). So learning is critical in organizations, and organizations need advice, support, and professional talent to maximize their investment in the development of employees and leaders. Consultants provide this expertise. Consultants apply learning theory and research to guide the design of effective learning interventions.

Consultants advise on methods of assessment to ascertain employees' needs for learning, and they devise ways for employees to balance technical, cognitive, and social skill development. They design and administer training to meet immediate technical needs and implement career development programs that prepare individuals to be ready for anticipated future technical and leadership needs (Diamante, 2011). The training may

http://dx.doi.org/10.1037/0000094-002
Learning Interventions for Consultants: Building the Talent That Drives Business, by M. London and T. Diamante

be modular, delivered in small units, such as online or in-person workshops on a particular topic. It may be experiential, with time for participants to practice and receive feedback on the job aimed at mastering particular competencies (Tannous, 2016).

Education for skill and competency learning is important, if not critical, for organizational change and development. Consultants need to know how learning experiences can add value to organizational change interventions and performance management (appraisal, feedback, and coaching). Consultants can help increase the capacity of individuals, teams, and organizations in the process of technological innovation, technology adoption, dynamic growth, and shifts in strategic direction.

The role of the learning professional and consultant has changed from designer and controller to facilitator and guide. Learning technologies together with organizational problem solving put the onus of learning and control of learning on the individual and team. The consultant becomes the designer, facilitator, assessor, and source of feedback to guide learning, and the learner takes responsibility for learning and learning outcomes.

Consultants have the advantage of computer-based learning technologies for cost-effective delivery of training programs. Technologies make education and information for learning and ongoing development available anytime, anywhere, and on any device. Moreover, technologies allow individuals and teams to control their own learning. Technology can catalyze the capability and speed of learning as learners share, question, think critically, and explore subject matter together.

Most learning is experiential and occurs on the job. Roughly 70% of learning occurs through direct experience, 20% through observing others, and 10% through structured learning programs (Lombardo & Eichinger, 2000). Considerable learning occurs informally through incidental events and serendipitous experiences (Marsick & Watkins, 2001). Facilitators of learning can help employees and leaders identify and create learning opportunities, formal and informal, planned and unplanned, blending different methods (Rabin, 2015). Learning programs can combine job experiences with assessment, feedback, coaching, modeling, and structured learning. Consultants integrate training with other interventions to develop learning communities, solve problems, and introduce continuous quality improvement programs. They may establish collaborative peer forums for participants to experiment with new work methods and share results.

Consultants as learning professionals work in diverse sectors of the economy including corporate, health and human services, education, entertainment, cultural institutions, municipalities, and the arts. Consultants add value to large and small for-profit, not-for-profit, and government organizations; geographically dispersed organizations; and multinational/cross-cultural organizations. Moreover, consultants work with both unskilled and skilled populations.

The term workplace *training* traditionally refers to the education employees receive to do their work now. The term *learning* refers to what happens during training and beyond as employees acquire and apply new skills and knowledge gained during training. Training includes structured learning activities that are aimed at learning specific concepts and acquiring targeted behaviors. The activities may be in a classroom or off-site workshop/conference facility setting, online, on the job, or a combination of settings. Training may take place within the organization or it may be delivered elsewhere, for instance, at a college or a training consulting firm. An instructor, who may be a training professional or an experienced employee or supervisor, provides information, guidance, testing, and coaching as employees practice and demonstrate their new knowledge and skills. Learning materials (e.g., textbooks, videos, websites) may be used.

Employees recognize the value of learning. Respondents to a survey of 1,800 employees in a wide range of companies said they spent approximately 17 hours per year in training (Osborn, 2016). The employees indicated that they would like to spend more time in training, and they believed that the more time they spend in training, the more effective they are on the job. Moreover, the respondents preferred "micro-learning"—training resources that might be 10 to 30 minutes per session. As on-the-go learning becomes more popular, employees will be more comfortable with this type of training (Osborn, 2016). However, consultants who are designing this type of training need to be cautious of do-it-yourself presentations. Electronic forms of learning delivery (e-learning), like any mode of learning, is only as good as the quality of the content, the fidelity of the presentation format, the ability of the facilitator, and the motivation and ability of the learners.

EXAMPLES OF CORPORATE APPROACHES TO EMPLOYEE LEARNING

Employers are adopting creative and cost-effective approaches to learning. Consider some examples from technology companies based on a study conducted by Wilson (2016). Salesforce uses an interactive customer learning platform for in-house sales account executive training. Building from a foundation of traditional face-to-face training, employees and their managers create individualized learning "journeys" to meet each employee's personal development needs and goals. The system tracks learning and relates learning needs to the accomplishments of each sales person, always with the aim to put customers first. Yelp emphasizes retaining talented employees through learning and development. Yelp executives actively mentor new recruits emphasizing that employee development is their key priority. In this way, employees are learning continuously with the support of their managers. Pandora recognizes that employees leave the company because of poor relationships with their immediate supervisor. An employee engagement survey tracks the strength of employee–manager relationships, and new managers are taught to coach, support, and manage their subordinates and rewarded for doing so. The company makes all manager training available online and on demand, with sessions taking less than 15 minutes to complete.

Facebook promotes respect and fosters a culture of continuous learning, personalizing learning experiences through many on-demand classes and career flexibility. The company recognizes that most learning happens organically within departments and is peer to peer and employee driven. The company's Engage Coaching program gives new managers one-to-one sessions with an executive coach to help them develop effective people management skills. The firm's Facebook Leadership in Practice (FLIP) program uses case studies, team building, and coaching circle exercises to give feedback and coaching from peers and executives to rising leaders. The coaching circles are groups of managers meeting in person or online for a designated time each week to practice listening to and supporting each other in developing new ways of approaching their current leadership challenges. Each group member takes a turn at describing current challenges, and the other members act as a board of advisors to share and take advantage of their expertise and experience. Facebook's Unconscious Bias program trains employees to recognize workplace bias and build productive relationships to create a culture of collaboration and continuous learning.

From the organization's standpoint, the purpose of employee learning should be business value (Wilson, 2016). The driver of learning should be a business problem, and the enabler of learning should be imaginative delivery. The opportunity to learn should be viewed by the organization and employees as an investment in the productive value of the employee—part of the firm's reward package that attracts and engages (and hence retains) employees while building individual capability.

CONSULTANTS' ROLES IN DESIGNING LEARNING INTERVENTIONS

Learning consultants may use measures of cognitive ability and/or personality to assess characteristics of current employees (Bertua, Anderson, & Salgado, 2005; Hogan, Barrett, & Hogan, 2007). They may conduct a needs analysis (Bowman & Wilson, 2008) in a department or the entire organization to identify skill and knowledge gaps, establish learning objectives, and design and deliver training programs. The consultants may measure and report the success of a training program—the degree to which employees learned what they were supposed to learn, assessed immediately following training, and the degree to which employees transferred their knowledge to the job.

Facilitators of learning may develop assessment methods to determine employees' readiness for new and more advanced assignments—for instance, readiness to be promoted to a managerial or executive position based on their leadership ability. The assessments may include observing employees in a range of exercises and tests, administered in person or online. A common method is the assessment center during which candidates for positions are assessed for hire or advancement potential based on their performance on behavioral tests and in business simulations (Thornton & Gibbons, 2009). Formative assessments give employees guidance to help them plan their development in relation to organizational needs. (These are in contrast to summative assessments, which are used to evaluate and make decisions about employees.) The assessment center assessors may observe participants prioritizing information, preparing for and delivering a presentation, seeking additional information, participating in a group discussion, and making decisions, often in interaction with other employees who are being assessed. Online assessments may include asking participants to react to recorded stimuli (e.g., video scenarios, e-mails, pop-up texts) or interact with people in real time (e.g., actors playing managers on the phone).[1]

Individual assessments are another method for determining developmental needs (Jeanneret & Silzer, 1998). The consultant may be asked to evaluate individual employees for various reasons—for instance, an executive wanting an opinion about a candidate for an important job or about a manager who is having performance problems. In conducting such assessments, the consultant identifies knowledge and skills important to the position in question and then creates or identifies methods that will lead to inferring suitability or developmental needs (Lowman, 2016). The assessments may include a set of tests; an interview with the executive; possibly observations of the executive in meetings, presentations, social settings, or other forums; and interviews with coworkers and/or customers or other contacts outside the organization. The consultant aggregates the results and draws informed conclusions about the individual. The consultant uses the assessment results to give feedback to the individual and coach him or her on setting goals for performance improvement and development (Gregory & Levy, 2015). The consultant may continue coaching the individual over time, following up with meetings and phone

---

[1]For more information on assessment centers, see the International Congress on Assessment Center Methods website (http://www.assessmentcenters.org).

calls, and collecting information later from others about the individual's abilities and performance for ongoing feedback and coaching (Diamante & Primavera, 2004; Natale & Diamante, 2005).

Designing Interventions to Support Organization Change

Organizations are constantly changing, and consultants need to have the tools to support the changes. Pressure for organizational change stems from economic, cultural, and technological events and innovations that require the acquisition of new knowledge and skills, both technical and managerial. Some changes are incremental and can be absorbed by offering employees training, for instance, to learn new software. Other changes can be radical or "frame breaking." They occur quickly and require major shifts in thinking and how work is performed. Consider the following examples of organizational change and input from learning consultants:

- An organization that operates in one country was acquired by a multinational organization in order to expand the business internationally. A consultant assessed managerial cultural sensitivity as part of providing training in cultural competence.
- A retailer shifted from bricks-and-mortar to online sales. A consultant helped the retailer adjust to the changes that resulted from the organization's new way of doing business.
- An international NGO trained field workers in emergency preparedness. The NGO hired a consultant to evaluate skill requirements and design and run training exercise.
- A multinational cosmetics firm aiming to be more innovative hired a consultant to develop brainstorming training experiences for business unit teams.
- A manufacturing company hired a consultant to organize problem-centered, team-building exercises. Executives assigned teams a real problem to work on, and the consultant facilitated the teams' progress and interactions.
- A learning consultant worked with a company's emergency management team to design online crisis management training, implement a

violence prevention initiative, and develop enhanced emotional and behavioral health educational programs.

- A consultant and technical trainers introduced new coding and tracking software; the consultant incorporated work–life management and stress reduction techniques to help employees deal with 24/7 access to information and a decreasing identity with a single company unit.

Learning Professionals as Coaches

Coaching employees one to one or in teams is another method for learning. Unlike training per se, where the goal is a targeted capability to perform a task or engage in a structured or well-defined job, coaching is providing feedback, serving as a sounding board, and offering advice and guidance. A meta-analysis that aggregated the results of 24 studies published from 2000 to 2014 showed that coaching has strong effects on improving leadership behaviors and skills, especially stress management, coping skills, and commitment to the organization (Sonesh et al., 2015). The background of coaches predicted outcomes. Some coaches were consulting psychologists, and others had managerial backgrounds in a variety of fields. Organizational outcomes were best when the coaches had a mix of backgrounds, some consulting psychologists and some with internal, business experience in management. As a highly personalized practice, coaching requires a tailored approach (Diamante, 2011). The number of coaching sessions is highly variable and dependent upon the circumstances, especially in high-stakes business situations or in highly complex, emotionally laden circumstances. Sonesh et al. (2015) recommended that coaches adopt a *person-centered approach* that assumes that the person being coached is his or her own best expert. The coach's role is to detect what a person needs, how ready the individual is to address challenges, what pace to take in working them through these challenges, and what "talking style" or counseling orientation to deploy (Goodstone & Diamante, 1998).[2]

---

[2] For resources on coaching, we recommend Simpson (2014) and Goldsmith, Lyons, and McArthur (2012).

LEARNING CONSULTANTS' COMPETENCIES AND AREAS OF EXPERTISE

One of the fundamental competencies for consultants is to understand the extent of organizational change and its implications for learning and human development. Consultants bring a set of values to the learning enterprise. These values include the desire to improve employees' work lives, an appreciation for the success of the organization, and an understanding of an organization's triple bottom line: profit, social responsibility (e.g., environmental sustainability), and employee engagement. Consultants take a systems perspective by recognizing how different functions and disciplines in an organization work together, and particularly how elements of the organization's human performance system, including training and development, contribute to organizational success. Consultants apply evidence-based practice by drawing on methods that have demonstrated value to organizational effectiveness as well as to individual and team learning. Learning professionals bring a humanistic perspective that embeds ethics in the training enterprise. Ethical practice entails communicating clearly to client organizations and employees what they can expect from the training, assessing learning outcomes, and giving feedback to employees to help them to improve and apply what they are learning.

Consultants engage with clients to solve human resources (HR) problems and address any and all areas of an organization. Training and development is often part of the solution. Consider the range of consultants' roles in organizations in Table 1.1. Any or all client engagements may entail learning as part, or a main function, of a consulting intervention. Although a learning program is certainly not a solution to all problems, often a consultation entails educating one or more employees, managers, executives, or teams to address specific issues and/or be prepared for future contingencies. Learning is fundamental to organizations because while innovations in learning modalities are always developing, learning is essentially about business results. Learning processes are often the compelling part of an intervention, but the value resides in behavior change that produces a positive impact on targeted outcomes.

Table 1.1

Consulting Initiatives and Learning Interventions

Consulting initiatives	Sample learning interventions for leaders
Establishing strategies (goals and objectives) and developing policy, procedure, and practices	Workshops on goal setting
Facilitating collaboration among individuals, teams and departments	Team-building exercises; training and team brainstorming aimed at innovation and problem solving; uncovering intrapersonal drivers of unproductive relations (and removing them); conflict mediation
Designing new organizational structures and work group configurations	Training in identifying and comparing best practices and establishing benchmark measures; identifying alternative business processes to improve organizational effectiveness; revealing group deficiencies and their cause(s); identifying technological enhancement for interpersonal exchange and consequent innovation
"Right sizing" the organization	Training in assessing needed talent and structuring jobs; getting professionally and emotionally ready to execute the initiative; supporting (counseling) affected employees; improving organizational communications so leadership is left with a beginning (and not an ending)
Improving organizational competency and competitiveness	Workshops on self-assessment and seeking feedback; competency "gap" analysis to bridge the current culture state to the planned future state; bringing a human capital perspective to situational or competitive analysis being discussed by management
Increasing efficiency and effectiveness of operations	Training in efficiency measurement and benchmarks for comparisons; ensuring that metrics motivate and do not eviscerate the workforce intention to achieve; engaging in talent assessment based on job requirements to be; and ensuring validation of selected or customized HR decision-making tools

Table 1.1
Consulting Initiatives and Learning Interventions (*Continued*)

Consulting initiatives	Sample learning interventions for leaders
Assessing and identifying talent (especially leadership talent at all levels of the organization)	Training in selection methods, such as interviewing (information gathering and use to make effective decisions); serving as an assessor in an assessment center; evaluating assessment tools; connecting talent selection with policy making, selection criteria, and promotional and development procedures; and establishing decision-making criteria based on EEO law and professional guidelines for employment selection and assessment
Providing feedback to and coaching leaders	Training leaders to give feedback and be more effective coaches; leading by example by being a transformational advisor; educating leadership on group dynamics, organizational health and well-being, motivation, and employee engagement
Determining directions for and implementing changes in process and culture	Training in understanding, measuring, and influencing organizational culture; building compelling communications; directing behavioral change; and linking HR practices to ensure support of business objectives
Tracking organizational climate	Training in interpreting and using organizational climate survey results; building a full understanding of employee engagement; clarifying how to optimize positive impact at organizational, business unit, and individual levels of analysis
Evaluating the success of interventions	Training in applied research design and use of results for future improvements; building cultures that embrace continuous improvement and the asking of questions that can upset the status quo for the sake of making the organization stronger
Readiness for organizational change in order to meet future needs and manage uncertainties	Training in assessing organizational environment, individual and systemic resistance to change, and how to impact behavior of others to catalyze movement toward a healthier state

19

Many consultants involved in training have an area of expertise that they developed during their career. Training is one of a range of consulting capabilities and experiences that center on organizational and individual change; performance and technology management; career development; and talent identification, which includes selection, testing, competency modeling, employee relations, litigation prevention, performance management and leadership development. Examples of areas for training are executive development, corporate governance, social responsibility, ethics, sales and marketing, project management, performance appraisal, giving and receiving feedback, implementation and integration of technology, antidiscrimination, diversity and EEO matters, cultural sensitivity, and general HR strategy and operations (including compliance with state and federal employment laws). Consultants may develop a reputation as excellent in one or more areas. Some consultants have prepackaged training programs or workshops that they can adapt to meet organizational needs; others apply their subject matter expertise in a more customized fashion.

A consultant who brings expertise in learning methods and one or more other subjects offers a powerful combination. A learning intervention may emerge as a way to solve a pressing business or performance problem, but this may not be obvious at the outset of the consultation. In time, the need for learning surfaces and the consultant may be asked to provide all or part of the learning content and delivery. As such, the consultant needs to have the knowledge and skill to work on all phases of learning and recognize how the learning intervention supports other elements of an organizational change initiative.

The Learning Consultant's Perspective

A consultant's role in learning interventions will likely entail working with other professionals, in particular, instructional designers, training professionals, and/or HR leaders. Learning professionals may collaborate with subject matter experts in fields such as risk management, law, sales and marketing, corporate social responsibility, and business ethics to craft learning events. Each of these professions offers unique perspectives to organizational challenges. The learning consultant's perspective adds value especially when it reflects a systemic approach to individual, team, and organizational change over time.

Consultants as learning professionals bring the following perspectives to needs analysis, design, implementation, and assessment of learning interventions:

- a multidisciplinary, broad range of views on adult learning and development drawing on social, personality, industrial, organizational, and experimental psychology;
- a recognition that learning interventions are not cure-alls but methods that can be structured to support and/or complement consulting efforts in order to accomplish client goals;
- a view that learning incorporates individual behavior change, team learning, and organizational level change;
- a concern for transfer of training—that is, that learning interventions need to need to be properly contextualized to benefit the organization;
- an understanding that the fidelity of training or its capacity to generalize to situations and responsibilities back on the job is critical;
- a desire to explore electronic technologies that can lead to creative, and sometimes disruptive, changes to employees' attitudes and behaviors;
- the ability to design learning interventions that promote discovery and innovation;
- a readiness to be involved in any or all stages of learning design and delivery, whether needs analysis, design, implementation, and/or assessment;
- an open mind and a desire to be innovative and creative—not necessarily repeating methods that worked in other consulting or organizational contexts; and
- a readiness to learn and change the solution path as a consultancy unfolds.

Salas, Tannenbaum, Kraiger, and Smith-Jentsch (2012) summarized expectations that executives and leaders have for a learning intervention. These are the elements that consultants want to provide as they support an organization's learning and development. Consultants and executives can discuss whether the firm (a) is invested sufficiently and wisely in training, (b) prioritizes training needs, (c) is clear about the competencies the organization needs to compete successfully, (d) has a learning environment that is conducive to learning, (e) is sending the right signals to employees about the value of learning to the organization, (f) is supporting growth in competencies that are transportable over time as new objectives and strategies are formulated, (g) provides evidence that the learning has produced positive outcomes, and (h) shows how the training investment relates to other elements of a high-performing, learning organization.

Consider what a learning consultant may be asked to do. The organization may want the consultant to develop employees so they can move from one project to another or participate on multiple project teams at one time, exhibit learning agility to adapt to new technologies and work methods quickly, be open to new ideas, work cooperatively with fellow employees in diverse disciplines, solve problems quickly, be innovative, integrate technological process with interpersonal skills, be flexible in their personal lives— able to balance work and nonwork responsibilities and interests—and/or be continuous learners, who are up-to-date on technology, the industry, and work methods.

Implementing a learning intervention requires

- *resources:* training materials and facilities, such as high-tech, "smart" classrooms with wireless Internet access, presentation technologies, and individual computers or tablets;
- *administration:* staff for setup, scheduling, and monitoring;
- *time:* for the trainers, facilitators, and learners;
- *beta testing:* trying the training on samples of learners who then provide reactions and test results as feedback to improve the training; comparing the training results with other forms of training or with performance without training, making adjustments to improve the learning experience;
- *train-the-trainer sessions:* training professionals or employees who will deliver the training and be first adopters and subject matter experts to guide new learners;
- *rollout:* delivering the training over time;

- *designing experiences:* in person or virtual delivery of learning experiences;
- *continuous improvement of learning methods:* changing methods to improve learning (e.g., if costly materials such as videos and voice-over PowerPoint presentations have been carefully constructed and tested, their positioning during the learning experience may be changed without altering the materials); and
- *innovation:* exploration of emerging technologies and software functionality as they increase efficiencies of learning delivery.

Learning consultants are well positioned to incorporate sensitive interpersonal matters to produce positive organizational change. In the following case of customer relations training, a learning consultant touched upon issues related to unconscious bias, person perception, and social stereotyping.

CASE 1.1: CUSTOMER SERVICE TRAINING

A metropolitan museum hired a learning consultant to design and implement a 1-day training program for all employees who had contact with visitors to the museum. A world-renowned cultural institution curating the world's contemporary and historical treasures, the museum was concerned that security guards and other employees did not have a sense of how they influenced the visitor experience. This need became evident after a major altercation between a security guard and an unhappy visitor.

All employees with visitor contact attended the program. The training emphasized the role of all employees in making a visit to the museum a memorable experience. The consultant developed a training module about dealing with difficult visitors that was entitled "What Could Go Wrong?" During the training, employees rated their job engagement on a series of items, including (a) the extent to which the work itself is engaging; (b) the extent to which this job is rewarding, relative to similar jobs held elsewhere; (c) employees' satisfaction with management; and (d) the extent to which the job should be rooted in making visitors happy. The consultant averaged the results and shared them with the participants in open discussion during the training session to establish a healthy dialogue.

The training emphasized the value of visitors' having a positive experience. Employees were shown web-based digital maps for visitors and innovations in the walking tour. The consultant felt that employees needed to appreciate the investment the museum was making to improve the visitor experience and increase visits to the museum. The training also informed employees about the measures the museum was using to monitor visits (e.g., feedback on headsets worn by visitors, and observations from stealth visitors mingling with real visitors to gain access to genuine reactions to exhibits).

During the training, to ensure that learning was taking place, the learning consultant asked employees to discuss how they would handle different scenarios of visitor interactions. During these discussions, the consultant highlighted the connections between the employees' feelings and making decisions on how to respond to visitors. The training emphasized visitor satisfaction and included good ways to handle unruly visitors.

Posttraining measures of success for the program were based on a survey that asked employees about the quality of the training as well as about perceptions of their jobs and their role in curating the visitor experience.

CONCLUSION

Consultants can offer an understanding of the individual, team, and organizational context and processes that are intertwined with needed learning. They recognize the short-term need for training and its long-term value for career and organizational development. In addition, the value of learning as a solution is strategically positioned in alignment with other talent management programs, practices, and policies. Consultants can provide the support and coaching employees need to learn and apply learning in often complex situations that go beyond what the need seemed to be at first blush—in this case, an example of customer service training.

In the next chapters, we review seminal research on the psychology of learning (Chapter 2); outline steps for developing learning interventions (Chapter 3); describe adaptive, generative, and transformative learning interventions (Chapter 4); describe a wide variety of learning technologies (Chapter 5); and recommend ways consultants can provide added value to individuals, teams, and total organizations (Chapter 6).

2

The Science of Learning and Development

Learning professionals apply training practices that research has shown to be effective—that produce positive results for individuals, teams, and organizations (Chen & Klimoski, 2007). Effective learning requires an alignment between individual-level and contextual aspects of the learning environment and employees' ability and desire to learn and transfer to the job. Salas, Tannenbaum, Kraiger, and Smith-Jentsch (2012) emphasized that training is a system embedded in an organizational context and that the best designed systems are consistent with organizational goals and strategies and have the support of human resources (HR) systems.

Technology is revolutionizing training (Li, 2016; Salas & Cannon-Bowers, 2001). The learning technologies that build on learning theory to improve learning include intelligent tutoring systems, simulations, multimedia systems, artificial intelligence, web-based training, voice-controlled

http://dx.doi.org/10.1037/0000094-003
Learning Interventions for Consultants: Building the Talent That Drives Business, by M. London and T. Diamante

interactive learning, virtual environments, and online groups for shared learning experiences.

A review of training and development research dating back to the early 1900s demonstrated the emergence of theory-driven research; the importance of the context for training and the characteristics of the trainee; new options for training design and delivery; the emergence of more reliance on self-regulated learning; a recognition that learning occurs outside the class or training room; and consideration of training's value at the individual, team, and organizational levels (Bell, Tannenbaum, Ford, Noe, and Kraiger, 2017). These trends are evident throughout this book as we focus on the role of the learning consultant. This chapter reviews seminal psychology-based research that is the foundation for effective learning processes.

WHAT WE KNOW ABOUT EFFECTIVE LEARNING METHODS

Training and development research generated useful knowledge that shows the effects of training antecedents on learning processes and outcomes. Chen and Klimoski (2007) cited research that shows the effects of boundary conditions that may limit or support the value of training. An example is the assumption that older employees have difficulty developing new knowledge and skills because they are not as motivated to learn, and others in the organization are not supportive due to stereotypes they hold about older adults' ability to learn (Maurer, Weiss, & Barbeite, 2003). Other research indicates the importance of training design for learners to explore new ideas as well as to learn what they need to know now (Morgan & Berthon, 2008). For instance, training that encourages exploration and recognizes the value of making mistakes as more effective than training that avoids trainees making errors (Schmidt & Ford, 2003).

Educational theory and research has demonstrated interactions between learners and learning methods. As an example, training that encourages exploration and not setting learning goals too early in the training process will be more effective for trainees who have higher levels of cognitive ability and openness to experience (Kanfer & Ackerman, 1989). Another example is that training is more effective when trainees decide on their own to participate in training rather than when they are assigned to training by their supervisors (Mathieu, Tannenbaum, & Salas, 1992). Cross-training employees so they learn each other's tasks can increase team learning outcomes (Marks, Zaccaro, & Mathieu, 2000).

The benefits of training are evident in studies that take multi-disciplinary, multilevel, and global perspectives. As Aguinis and Kraiger (2009) reported, the benefits of training can be maximized by careful needs assessment and evaluation of learners' capability and motivation. Participants respond favorably to learning that they apply immediately to do their job better and is supported by their supervisor and coworkers. Learning opportunities help recruit and retain talent because they convey to employees that the organization cares about their professional and career development. Training can be made more cost-effective and can improve learning when managers are held accountable (and rewarded) for supporting their subordinates' learning, and when employees are evaluated and rewarded for using training knowledge and skills on the job.

Building Self-Regulation Into Learning

Consultants can design interventions to improve trainees' control over their own learning. Trainees' performance can be increased when they are prompted to self-regulate, especially for trainees who are already high in self-efficacy (Sitzmann, Bell, Kariger, & Kanar, 2009). Self-regulation allows trainees to guide their goal-directed behavior over time as situations change. Self-paced technology gives trainees more control over their learning experience within the limits of the instructions. Trainees who do not take full advantage of self-pacing capability may do so because they fail to regulate themselves well. They do not accurately assess their current knowledge and abilities and so do not devote sufficient time to learning. Prompts or questions built into the instructions can encourage self-regulation, such as self-monitoring learning activities and self-evaluation of learning. Questions written by the training professional are posed by the training software, and the software uses the trainees' answers to individualize the learning pathway. Questions might require a response to work situations to simulate challenges or assess knowledge/skill acquisition throughout a training program using quizzes or check-ins. The key is requiring success before the learners move to the next level or module.

Sitzmann et al. (2009) found that self-regulation can be increased through a learning intervention, and that this can improve performance on basic knowledge and strategic skills. They studied adult learners participating in an online course on how to use a computer-based learning system. The goal was to learn basic performance on the system—the fundamental principles and operations. Ten modules with text and video demonstrations were presented. Each module covered a different feature of the system (e.g., a chat room module). In the experimental group, trainees were asked questions about their self-monitoring and self-evaluation as they proceeded through each module (e.g., compare your current knowledge and skills with the training goal). As an incentive, trainees who passed final test questions received a certificate of completion with a copy sent to their employer's HR department. The training prompts improved performance over time.

Learning Theories That Underlie Adaptive, Generative, and Transformative Learning

Adaptive, generative, and transformative learning derive from several related theories. Kraiger (2008) distinguished between *objectivist* and *constructivist* learning. Objectivist learning is instructor driven. This approach is fine for adaptive learning. Social constructivist learning is learner centered, with consultants creating meaningful learning environments, real-world simulations, short cases, and problem-solving exercises. This is more generative learning, and could be transformative. Examples of social constructivist learning would be interactive experiences with peer mentoring and collaborative discussion forums centered on team assignments. The learning experience might use social media such as chat rooms, community building social media (e.g., Twitter, Instagram, Facebook), discussion boards, blogs, shared online workspaces, and gaming. Moreover, vicarious learning is often overlooked and requires attention in an organizational context.

Individuals absorb and apply new concepts as they collaborate. This can occur in ad hoc groups—learners participating together, understanding and practicing new skills and knowledge, and supporting each other in the process with the guidance of the trainer/consultant. At the team level, people who work together regularly participate in the learning process and then discuss their interactions as they learn, invent, and incorporate new processes, becoming a more collaborative team that produces positive outcomes.

Kraiger (2008) and Vygotsky (1978) defined the concept of social cognition that underlies generative and transformative learning. Learners who are collaborating discuss, interpret, create, integrate, and conceptualize concepts and experiences. Learners take an active role in the learning process. Social cognition is especially appropriate for transformative learning, during which learners fashion the learning process and the outcomes as they face new challenges and formulate new goals. The consulting psychologist incorporates social cognitive processes as ways to facilitate the learning process. The consultant may be a mentor, coach, instructional designer, and educator. At the individual level, the goal(s) may be increased mindfulness, being more attuned to others and the environment, learning more about oneself and others, being more collaborative, unearthing and resolving conflicts constructively, and/or other dimensions of interpersonal behavior. These outcomes occur as by-products of generative training methods, which may also be focused on specific corporate objectives centering on new policies, strategies, goals, and/or technologies. At the team level, intact work groups experience the learning together. The consultant helps the team recognize, practice, and codify the learning to sustain new teamwork processes. For instance, in learning how to collaborate more effectively, team members may establish a routine for time set aside to discuss what they perceive about team members' interaction, list possible barriers to progress, and consider ways to overcome them.

Knowles (1975, 1984), in his theory of adult learning (*andragogy*), argued that people become self-directed learners as they accumulate learning experiences. Over time, depending on their ability and motivation to learn and available resources and encouragement for learning, they recognize that ongoing development is beneficial for job performance. They realize that they draw on learning to solve problems in their jobs and lives in general. Their motivation for learning increases, particularly learning that has immediate applicability. As such, people want to be involved in planning their learning and evaluating what they learned, including learning from mistakes.

Mature learners understand how to apply their learning to solve problems rather than focus just on learning different topics or concepts. This has implications for designing learning interventions beyond mere memorization, including explaining why what they are learning is valuable and how the learning can be used. Those who reach the level of generative, self-directed learners may prefer to learn at their own pace and draw on each other for advice and collaboration, with the trainer as a facilitator. Online learning is particularly useful for applying Knowles's adult learning theory. It allows self-pace and self-direction, provides opportunities for exploration and collaboration with other learners and experts, and can include problem solving in realistic simulations and/or organizational challenges posed by executives.

Wittrock (1992), an educational psychologist, described generative learning based on a neural model of brain functioning. Individuals participate in learning in ways that help them form understanding in relation to the environment. They learn to recognize patterns of thought and behaviors. Once recognized, the consultant who is facilitating the learning can guide the participants in forming new patterns of thought and behaviors. This may be in line with corporate goals for the training—for example, for supervisors to use online monitoring systems to track employees' productivity and to empower employees to track and improve their own productivity. The role of the consultant is to facilitate the establishment of new neural networks—thought patterns that give rise to new behavior patterns. At the team or organizational level, members' individual thought patterns need to change as the team, or the organization as a whole, establishes new behavioral patterns that become part of the team's or organization's culture.

Forming new behavioral patterns in complex environments likely requires forgetting and replacing old knowledge and behaviors. Adaptive learning may require overriding neural networks to establish new standard responses to predictable situations. When new information, procedures, or behaviors are not sufficiently stored in memory, they are likely to be "forgotten" (Bartlett, 1932; Bjork, 1970; Danziger, 2008; Hardt, Nader, & Nadel, 2013). Forgetting may also occur if other events and information override or interfere with the learned material, or if the individual did not have a chance to practice and/or apply the instructions soon enough after training (M. Anderson, Bjork, & Bjork, 1994; Hardt et al., 2013). There could have been too much to learn too quickly, or perhaps learned material was not sufficiently cogent for the individual to bother learning. People may "forget" because they did not want to learn in the first place—maybe because the employee did not like the trainer and forgetting was a covert act of insubordination—or because the training was unpleasant—as learning math or statistics is for some people, especially if the educator is incompetent and/or fails to relate effectively to the learner. Generative learning requires the ability to apply learned material in new and different ways in relation to complex, often changing conditions. Old behaviors may no longer be applicable, or they may be applicable in some cases and not in others. Confusion from unforeseen situations may interfere with learned behaviors. Training may be of little value without time to embed learned material in memory and then draw on it in different ways to meet changing conditions.

Kolb (1976, 1981, 2015; Kolb, Osland, & Rubin, 1995a, 1995b) has provided a fine-tuned approach to adult learning. His now well-known and extensively researched model of experiential learning is based around a cycle of (a) concrete experience, (b) reflective observation, (c) abstract conceptualization, and (d) active exploration. (For a good summary of Kolb's work and other major theories of adult development, see Marsick, Nicolaides, & Watkins, 2014.) Learning professionals can apply this cycle to adaptive, generative, and transformative learning. The stages of learning provide consultants with ideas for designing and implementing the learning process that create opportunities for adaptive, generative, and transformative learning. Consultants begin by answering the question of whether adaptive, generative, transformative, or some combined form of learning is needed. Then, they consider how learners can be guided through concrete experience, reflective observation, abstract conceptualization, and active exploration.

Ways to Maximize Transfer of Training

Educational research links learning to brain function and learning methods that promote transfer of training to work settings; this has implications for the design of learning interventions (National Research Council, 2000). Learners must initially acquire basic knowledge. Knowledge that relies too heavily on context (i.e., cases about problems in specific situations) can reduce transfer to other situations. Learners may need clear explanations of how what they learned in one situation can be applied in other contexts. Too much abstract learning (e.g., just memorizing facts and methods) is not good either, since learners may need help applying abstract concepts. Applying learning is an active, dynamic process, often entailing a sequence of trials, assessments, feedback, and reflection. Employees bring their prior experiences to a learning intervention. Prior learning can improve later learning or restrict it, depending on whether prior learning is recognized, compatible with, and incorporated into the training. For example, not recognizing the reason for work outcomes could be a barrier to adopting new methods. In addition, reflecting on possible scenarios ("What if" problem solving) can increase learners' flexibility in adapting new knowledge and skills to changing conditions.

Value of a Needs Analysis Before Designing a Learning Intervention

Evaluating individual employees' competencies and needs for development is a necessary first step in a learning design. Recognizing that each person is unique when it comes to evaluation for lifelong learning, Kraiger and Wolfson (2011) recommended assessments and support systems for organizationally relevant as well as lifelong learning competencies. Consultants can use these techniques to evaluate employees' learning needs periodically, as they move into different career stages and consider competencies they need for today and the future. Learning programs need to be aligned with the client system of HR management. Also, learning programs can be a central part of an organizational culture change initiative.

At the organizational level, consultants can ask clients about their short and long-term goals and how a learning support system can contribute to these goals. Job and task analyses evaluate competencies that support effective job performance and future development opportunities (being able to learn to learn). This is followed by analyses of individuals in the organization—identifying who needs training and measuring individual dispositions to learning (motivation to learn; learning style preferences; ability to self-manage learning opportunities, including receiving and using feedback; and ability to make good decisions about where and how to locate learning resources). Kraiger and Wolfson (2011) suggested using the Effective Lifelong Learning Inventory (ELLI) developed by Crick and Yu (2008). This measures respondents' beliefs about how they learn, their curiosity, and whether they can learn how to learn. Kraiger and Wolfson also suggested asking respondents whether they believe there is value in participating in specific learning experiences such as a public speaking course, a leadership seminar, or a database software course.

Bedwell, Weaver, Salas, and Tindall (2011) advised distinguishing between *task work* (what people need to accomplish their jobs) and *teamwork* (skills people need to collaborate across functions, disciplines, organizations, and geographic boundaries). Task work competencies include knowledge of new technology and software and adaptability to be effective in dynamic work environments. Teamwork requires critical social thinking, intercultural competence, and shared leadership, possibly with different team members serving as leader when their knowledge, skills, and background are needed.

Distinguishing Between Formal and Informal Learning

Methods for adult learning include both formal (organizationally sponsored and culturally aligned training) and informal interactions during the normal course of work, as well as incidental learning, which is a by-product of work interactions (Marsick & Watkins, 1990; Bedwell et al., 2011). Formal methods are likely to be technology enhanced, drawing on multimedia and various forms of e-learning including simulations and games (e.g., Second Life; see Chapter 5, this volume, for more information about simulations, games, and other learning technologies). Technology can provide just-in-time training, making skills training available when and where it is needed through mobile and computer-based devices. Mobile delivery of training has been used for all types of training—technical, new hire orientation, core competencies, leadership development, and compliance (C. Anderson, 2016).

Another formal means of learning is *mentoring*, which includes assigning less experienced employees to more experienced employees who can model intercultural competence, adaptability, and leadership, among other critical skills. Of course, mentoring occurs informally as well. There are recent developments where "reverse mentoring" is explored to orient experienced managers with the phenomenological work–life understanding of less experienced employees who may be new entrants to the workforce. Technology can help here as well. Embodied conversational agents can deliver just-in-time information, for instance, computer-generated avatars with human mannerisms that interact with the learner providing verbal and nonverbal cues (Bedwell et al., 2011).

Learning Research as a Guide for the Future of an Organization and Its Employees

Kraiger (2014) noted that there has been a steady progression of the transfer of responsibility for learning from the supervisor who showed employees how to do their work to the learners of today. The workforce as learners are personally responsible for determining the knowledge and skills they need to acquire in order to do their jobs, regardless of whether they work in brick-and-mortar settings or in remote settings apart from a supervisor. Kraiger (2014) noted that although the trend is toward more self-guided learning online, trainees still need support before, during, and after learning. Employees who are inexperienced in navigating career success are not likely to recognize what they need to know and when. Learners need time to explore, to experiment, and to absorb learning content. Additionally, they need to know how to infer rules, principles, and strategies that apply to performing work tasks on their own. Trainees who participate in the design of training and who voluntarily participate in training are more likely to be more motivated to persist through the training and to apply what they learn on the job than those who are assigned to training without much explanation to understand its purpose and value (Bell & Kozlowski, 2010). Moreover, training is likely to transfer to the job when (a) situational constraints are removed, (b) trainees have a chance to apply the training soon after they learned the material, and (c) supervisors and coworkers are supportive and reward newly learned behaviors (Kraiger, 2014).

TEAM LEARNING

Since much work in organizations gets done in teams, learning consultants need an understanding of how teams learn—how individuals learn to work together to accomplish tasks. Team training, like individual learning, works within the larger organization in which the team exists. Training probably will not be effective, or at least not as effective as it could be, without taking into account situational expectations and conditions and task and team member characteristics. Team development begins with forming the team and establishing the structure (role assignments and reporting relationships) and processes (forums for discussions and getting work done). There are three conditions for calling a group a *team* (Hackman, 2001; Lowe, 2016). First, the team needs the right people—those who have experience and knowledge that is necessary to accomplish the team's goals. Second, the team must be "real," that is the members must be interdependent, know each other, and recognize the expertise that each member brings to the team. Moreover, the members must be committed to stay on the team to ensure its stability at least for sufficient time to accomplish the team's work. Third, the team must have clear goals that members understand.

Once these elements are established, team members need to know how to work collaboratively, especially when the demands of the task are high (e.g., tight deadlines; complex work among members representing different functions, disciplines, and experiences). Also, team demands and training depend on the stage of the team process (Hackman, 2001; Silberstang & Diamante, 2008; Wageman, Hackman, & Lowe, 2005). At the outset, members need to have information about each other and the task. As work progresses, members need to know how to participate in elements of the team process, for instance, to use technology for communication, share ideas, brainstorm without evaluating each other, and give each other feedback about their behaviors without attacking their personal characteristics. As work is concluded, members need training in how to reflect on their process and determine methods for future interaction that will improve team effectiveness. Team knowledge-building processes are important for successful collaborative problem solving. Consultants can facilitate team knowledge-building during problem solving by helping the team recognize and repeat effective processes.

Studying problem solving in NASA's Mission Control Center, which is responsible for controlling the International Space Station, Fiore, Wiltshire, Oglesby, O'Keefe, and Salas (2014) interviewed team members about the complex problems they dealt with that required collaboration among individuals and teams. Given the vast number of interconnected elements within and across the technical systems, as well as the high degrees of uncertainty and shifting task priorities, team members needed to go beyond their individual areas of technical and systems expertise to develop situational and task-relevant strategies for coordination and problem solving. Team members needed to expand their own knowledge continuously. Teams needed to develop shared problem-solving strategies such as team information exchange, knowledge sharing, generation of alternative solutions to problems, team evaluation and negotiation of alternatives, and team planning processes. They needed to monitor their progress to stay on track or adapt and reframe problems and strategies as situations changed. Some knowledge learning came from individual team members applying and sharing their expertise to contribute to the team's development (called "Internalized Team Knowledge"). Other knowledge came from the creation of strategies and processes that could be repeated as similar problem cues emerged in the future (called "Externalized Team Knowledge"). Teams learned interaction patterns associated with problem solving elements (cues), which could be events that occurred, recognizable trends, or methods of resolving uncertainty. Problem solving was successful when plans were sufficiently detailed and pertinent to the problem, and the planning processes and execution were efficient.

A team of experts does not ensure that the team will be collaborative. Team-focused training can improve collaboration, team performance, and effectiveness (Lacerenza & Salas, 2014). Initial barriers that make collaboration difficult include lack of planning and organizational support, lack of technologies for effective communication, and members' lack of collaborative experiences across team and organizational boundaries, as well as individual team members' lack of readiness to collaborate. Lacerenza and Salas (2014) recommended ways to avoid these barriers. Before team training starts, conduct an analysis of the team needs to identify the necessary teamwork competencies. Analyze the team task components and complexity. Identify characteristics of the team members (their individual competencies, experience in team work, and their experience working together as a team). The consultant should also examine the extent to which the organizational climate supports collaboration and learning. Develop team training content based on the competencies needed for collaboration. Adopt training delivery methods that fit the training content. Use information-based training methods to convey declarative knowledge, use demonstration-based methods to train new procedures, and practice-based methods for solving problems in uncertain and changing environments. Prepare team development aids such as clear, concise feedback throughout training and later during team interactions. Debrief situations with the team, and train leaders to be coaches for individual and team development. Evaluate team training by measuring reactions, learning behavior, and results, with measures at the individual and team level, and evaluate performance during multiple time periods as training progresses and after training. Promote transfer of team training by providing opportunities for teams to use their teamwork skills on the job, encouraging networking among employees.

Learning in Virtual Teams

Virtual teams are those whose members are in different locations, possibly in different countries across time zones, cultures, and languages. In addition to dealing with differences in disciplines, experiences, and personalities, team members communicate electronically. They may not even speak each other's languages and may rely on cloud-based translation software. These differences increase the stress on the team and further the value of continuous learning to work cooperatively.

Training for virtual teams needs to account for modes of communication—the processes and routines the team uses to meet and collaborate electronically—and ways to be sure everyone is on the same page with respect to goals, deadlines, roles, expectations for each team member, and accomplishments of each team member. This is easier when each team member has a specific task and the outputs of the team members merely need to be combined or performed sequentially with the input from one team member used before the next. However, complex tasks that require interaction among individuals who apply their unique expertise in a coordinated and collaborative way increase the demands on the members and the leader (Lacerenza, Zajac, Savage, & Salas, 2014). Mechanisms for teamwork include shared drives for sharing information and contributing to documents, discussion forums for expressing opinions, and online chat rooms for subgroups of team members to discuss issues. Teams can learn to use these to improve collaboration and produce timely outcomes. Training methods for virtual teams include training and practice in using the technology, problem-solving games and exercises, and time to reflect on group processes (what's working and what can be improved; Ferrazzi, 2014).

Team Readiness to Learn

Teams are more likely to learn when they recognize that there is a need to change and members are open to working differently. Learners in team settings are sensitive to the demands and concerns of other team members and the organization as a whole (London & Sessa, 2007). Team members interact with other teams within and outside the organization to access resources and to understand expectations others may have of them.

Communication patterns within a team are likely to influence the team's readiness to learn. These include discussing difficult issues (e.g., areas of disagreement among team members; feelings of uncertainty; and lack of information, knowledge, or expertise they need to do their work). Consultants can strengthen a team's ability to communicate effectively, learn, and achieve its goals by helping the team to recognize cues for change, such as lack of knowledge and skills that are holding the team back. Also, consultants can encourage the team to respond to the demands in the organizational environment, rather than ignore these demands, and to understand cultural norms and differences among the individual team members (Sessa & London, 2006; Silberstang & London, 2009). Cues that signal the need to learn come in the form of data or information, for instance, that the team's progress is slow, objectives or milestones remain unmet, and/or the dynamics in the team are not enhancing execution. Other cues for learning might be customer service complaints, malfunctioning equipment, uncoordinated emergency responses, or team members raising various concerns about how problems are being managed and resources allocated. The more these cues are explicit and discussed, the more the team is likely to be ready to learn—to listen to feedback, try new approaches, and incorporate ideas from others including the learning consultant as team facilitator. It is important not to ignore or miss business metrics from sources *outside* the organization to identify learning needs *inside* the organization.

The more the team is able to respond to changes in the organizational environment, ponder data, and revise routine operations to meet changing demands, the more its members will want to learn new ways of behaving. In addition, the more the team is able to discuss interpersonal dynamics that occur during team interactions, the more members will understand each other's cultural and educational backgrounds. This can lead to heightened levels of openness to new information and ideas. Communication facilitated by a learning consultant can build rapport and take advantage of the different disciplines and experiences that team members bring.

ORGANIZATIONAL LEARNING

Just as individuals learn to work together effectively and efficiently in teams, individuals and teams form organizations. *Organizational learning* refers to how the structure and processes in the organization adapt to meet changing demands from competition, consumers, technology, the economy, stockholders, funders, and the workforce. Learning ultimately involves individual employees at all levels of the organization. This learning is derived from having experiences that form employees' ability to adapt and transform the way they work together in order to compete. Organizations need to learn continuously to remain competitive and to grow (Senge, Kleiner, Roberts, Ross, & Smith, 2014).

Formal training in the elements of teamwork and technical aspects of operations is often a part of ongoing, internal transformation. However, many of the factors that influence continuous learning are informal. Studying a variety of companies, Tannenbaum (1997; Eddy, Tannenbaum, Lorenzet, & Smith-Jentsch, 2005) identified nine factors that influence and support organizational learning:

- be open to new ideas so learners are motivated to take chances,
- provide opportunities to learn (e.g., assign employees to challenging tasks),

- encourage coworkers to support each other,
- have high performance expectations,
- encourage supervisors to support learning,
- tolerate mistakes,
- provide technology and supplies that support learning,
- encourage learners to take risks if they are unsure, and
- be aware of the big picture (e.g., how learning contributes to team and organizational goals).

The following case shows how learning interventions can address pervasive organizational changes. What initially seemed to be helping employees to telecommute led the consultants to develop learning interventions to support new ways of interacting and address employees' insecurities due to challenges of cost reductions and goals to improve profitability. This shows that what seems to be the need at first blush may just scratch the surface.

CASE 2.1: LEARNING AND ORGANIZATION CHANGE

As a result of a harsh business environment, a Fortune 500 financial services firm took a close look at its operations and decided to reduce fixed costs by eliminating some of its office space. This meant that some staff would need to work remotely, from home or on the road visiting clients, and use shared space when they needed to come to the office. About 350 employees were expected to work remotely. This shift to a partially remote workforce represented a marked cultural change for this conventional organization. Employees recognized that the business was experiencing financial trouble, and the increased pressure to "do more with less" became the corporate mantra. In fact, management and employees alike spoke openly about the draconian cuts underway (i.e., staff reductions, reduced travel, giving up the company fleet of cars). However, these changes did not help morale. The CEO discussed these issues with the company's chief learning officer (CLO). The CLO decided that employees needed a learning intervention that would smooth the transition and maintain performance.

The CLO felt that the cost of hiring two external learning consultants would be justified if they could design a training intervention that would help staff members who would be working remotely to learn how to be effective and feel better about the new arrangement. The external consultants began by interviewing a sample of the people affected. They quickly discovered that employees' immediate concerns were about losing their jobs to automation, outsourcing, or not being visible daily to their bosses and coworkers. Many employees were concerned about how to organize their time, how often to report to the office either electronically or in person, and how to demonstrate that they were working when they were not in the office. The company had clear performance goals, for instance, sales and time spent with clients. But there were many other aspects of the positions that were less visible, including completing forms and making cold calls to prospective customers. Employees were also concerned that they would not be as engaged in discussions about corporate strategies, ideas, and referrals without being in the office every day.

Given these concerns, the CLO and consultants developed a 1-day training program that gave participants a chance to discuss their concerns and to learn about ways that they could stay engaged and be productive while working remotely. The training, led by one of the consultants in small groups at different company locations, included videos of employees at other companies that had implemented remote work for many of their employees. The training also included opportunities for participants to share ideas about how they could be productive working remotely. The CLO's goal was to communicate the benefits of the change and build buy-in. The training highlighted a major benefit—that the employees would have more freedom to integrate work with their personal lives. If they needed time for a doctor's appointment or to care for a sick family member, they could more easily arrange their schedule.

The training was supplemented by a new company website for employees to share experiences, chat with team members, recognize accomplishments, schedule online meetings, and reserve space in the office. A separate workshop was developed for supervisors to learn about and discuss the challenges of leading a remote work team. Follow-up workshops were held using online learning. The CLO included items in the annual employee survey about remote work.

One goal of the training was to shift the mentality of the affected workforce away from job uncertainty and toward building security through their productivity. To this end, essential features of all jobs were reiterated and linked to strategic business goals. The online training focused on how to set goals, measure results, and build employee engagement even if face time was not frequent. The use of results and reported progress was central to the training. Managers were trained on communicating support for work being done to make sure employees did not feel alone or isolated. The training emphasized the psychological ramifications of feeling isolated, unsupported, and without a sense of belonging. Managers' responsibility was to keep their team members psychologically connected. Training for employees emphasized self-sufficiency for getting the information they needed to be successful. This included asking their managers for information, resources, and/or time. The training suggested ways employees could compensate for the absence of impromptu conversations.

The responsibility for establishing reasonable, attainable goals was shared mutually by managers and employees, but accountability for getting things done rested squarely on the shoulders of the employees. One interesting component of the training was a module on the use of electronic communications. This addressed the risks when working virtually of miscommunication and misinterpretation of information in e-mails.

Overall, the training addressed how work was changing at the individual and team levels. Employees considered how they could work with each other productively in the new environment. Finally, career development was addressed by explaining how a remote employee could be identified as high potential and move up in the organization. An interesting twist on this program was the invitation to include remote employees as leaders of periodic online workshops. Hearing from fellow employees about how to be productive resonated with affected employees. By stepping away and transferring training skills to originally highly resistant participants, the CLO and consultants were able to keep the material current and deal with problems as they arose, such as software issues, availability of shared office space, and managers scheduling sufficient face time with their team members.

CONCLUSION

To summarize key points from the training literature reviewed here:

- Consultants can assess learners' motivation to learn.
- Training design should be based on learning theory.
- Learning theories support adaptive, generative, and transformative learning (see Chapter 4 for associated learning methods).
- Learning interventions should be integrated with other HR practices, such as selection and performance management.
- Learning should incorporate interpersonal factors such as coworker and supervisor support.
- Training should recognize moderators, such as accountability, that improve learning.
- Learning technologies can adapt to learners' abilities.
- Learning outcomes should be measured, and the benefits documented.
- Teams need to be ready to learn.
- Learning can occur in virtual teams.
- Teams and organizations can be learning units and be able to adapt and transform themselves and their environments.

The case showed that a challenge for learning consultants is to be willing to go deeper to understand root causes and design learning that can benefit individuals and the organization. If the CLO and, subsequently, the two learning consultants had not dug deeper, the CLO might have been content with a simple communication to employees about the office space change. This would have missed an opportunity to address employees' concerns before they emerged in a dysfunctional way later, perhaps as high turnover or poor performance. Instead, the consultants took a more comprehensive approach to a transformative change in how work gets done in the organization. They also designed follow-up workshops to recognize that this is a long-term process that requires changing individual and team behavior. Chapter 3 turns to steps consultants can take in designing learning interventions.

3

A Five-Step Process for Designing and Delivering Learning Interventions

A learning engagement generally has five steps: (a) an initial needs analysis perhaps based on the client's perception of need; (b) contracting, which may call for a more in-depth needs analysis and could result in renegotiating the contract depending on the results; (c) learning design and development; (d) implementation; and (e) evaluation. A learning consultant may be brought in for one or more of these steps, and likely all of them if the consultant is involved in comprehensive design and implementation of a learning intervention. This chapter describes each of the steps (see Table 3.1), with examples and recommendations for action. Although we offer a step-wise, sequential process, the consultant should not fear ambiguity and instead embrace opportunities to rethink, reexamine and reimagine interventions when entering a client system.

http://dx.doi.org/10.1037/0000094-004
Learning Interventions for Consultants: Building the Talent That Drives Business, by M. London and T. Diamante

Table 3.1

Five-Step Process for Learning Interventions

Step	Key points
Needs analysis	Hold an initial meeting with the client to discuss the client's view of the learning gap and need for training or other form of learning intervention.
	Collect additional information by interviewing, surveying, and/or observing individuals and teams at work to understand, validate, or refocus the client's perspective.
	Recognize the needed mix of adaptive, generative, and/or transformative learning.
Contracting	Propose learning solution, including more extensive needs analysis (if required), expected learning outcomes, content, mode of delivery, resource requirements, timeline, cost, conducting a pilot program, the possibility of revising the intervention (which may require revising the contract based on additional information and the success of the pilot), and follow-up evaluation.
Learning design and development	Develop the content and mode of delivery that match organizational needs; draw on a wide range of delivery modes (Chapter 4) and technologies (Chapter 5).
Implementation	Test the program, revise as necessary, and deliver as per contract.
Evaluation	Assess effectiveness and return on investment.

STEP 1: PROBLEM REVIEW AND LEARNING NEEDS ANALYSIS

This initial stage involves determining consulting goals and whether learning is needed for information, skills, or knowledge acquisition; for increasing the work capacity of individuals and teams; and/or for developing the organization as a whole. The initial needs analysis is comparable to a clinical intake interview that is conducted before the client and the therapist decide to proceed. This leads to a contract that sets clear expectations between the client and the consultant before an additional, more detailed needs analysis take place. Then a more extensive contract may be negotiated to design and implement a learning intervention based on the needs analysis. The contract should include a postintervention evaluation to determine if the participants achieved the learning objectives. The evaluation may suggest a contract for follow-up interventions or implementing the intervention for other units in the organization.

When the consultant is first called, the client is likely to have an indication of need, although the latter may look to the former to recommend the best way to achieve the learning-dependent business goal. Consultants may have to compete for the contract by submitting a proposal, or the client may approach the consultant directly, perhaps based on prior experience with the consultant, the consultant's reputation, or a recommendation from others internal or external to the organization. Social media is now a powerful driver of resources as the backgrounds, jobs held, and qualifications of consultants are in full view of the client.

The consultant's reputation may attract clients who want to bring a workshop experience to the organization. In such cases, the consultant has the solution (a training program or workshop) in search of problems. Consultants who specialize in specific challenges may develop a reputation for such services and be contacted by clients to deliver their program, perhaps after some customization to the client's needs and expectations. The consultant can analyze the need from an organizational standpoint (e.g., how will the training benefit the organization, department, and/or individuals?). Also, the consultant can obtain information about the context—the organization's history, problems that have occurred recently, corporate goals, organization structure, and other conditions and situations that may influence how the training is constructed and delivered. The consultant can explain the value of a proposed learning program, provide examples of how well it has worked elsewhere, and explain why it should be similarly successful in the new context.

Some clients are demanding and may insist on a specific learning intervention. In doing so, they are likely to have a purpose in mind, and therefore may not view a broader range of questioning to be within the scope of the consultancy. The consultant may have to be tactful by suggesting that a needs analysis—or even a more modest discussion about need—would be valuable. Indeed, the client may just want to schedule in-person training sessions or purchase online training without much discussion about why it is needed or how much impact the client expects. In such cases, the consultant can explain to the client that the training will likely be of greater value if the consultant understands the client's expectations and understands the context for the training. However, this takes a bit of professional willpower and tact when a lucrative contract is in the offing.

The match between the training content and the organization's culture is important to the success of the learning experience. The consultant can inquire about and judge the fit between the requested training and the organization's culture and performance management processes. The client may want the training to be a focal point for an organizational culture change, for instance, to help move from an autocratic to a more participative style of management. However, the behaviors that are the focus of the training should match other elements of the human performance system. For instance, a program that trains supervisors to support their subordinates' career development will not be of much value if there is little room for advancement, and if supervisors are not evaluated and rewarded for being coaches and developers to their subordinates.

Need for Adaptive, Generative, and/or Transformative Learning

A consultancy begins with a needs analysis to determine learning objectives and outcome measures (e.g., trainees' attitudes, behaviors, and performance; team development; and/or organizational change). Needs analysis involves more than asking individuals what they need to learn, since they are not necessarily the best judges of learning needs (Bell & Kozlowski, 2002). Needs analysis may include asking individuals about whether knowledge or skill training could enhance their performance. The consultant may also use various individual assessments to evaluate current knowledge. The consultant can analyze employees' educational background, job experiences, and prior participation in training programs to assess the skills and knowledge resident in a team or organization. The client may have a vision for strategic goals that will require different skill sets and ways of working that have implications for training. Learning consultants help organizations diagnose skill gaps relative to organizational objectives and estimate learning needs to help the organization implement strategies to accomplish its objectives.

The results of the needs analysis will determine whether the training design needs to foster adaptive, generative, and/or transformative learning (London & Sessa, 2006, 2007; see also the Introduction to this volume for definitions of these terms). The need may be to teach a specific skill (adaptive learning). Alternatively, the need may be for individuals' and/or teams' generative learning for continued professional and career development. The goal may to engender transformative learning for frame-breaking changes of behavior and work relationships that respond to evolving needs and opportunities in the organization, industry, or profession. As such, the learning outcomes may be amorphous and, as a result, difficult to measure or observe especially over short periods of time. However, the desired outcomes of transformative learning may be evident when the organization faces a major challenge, whether an emergency or an opportunity. Learning needs expressed as competitive organizational outcomes can be reflected in how the intervention is designed, delivered, and assessed.

The desired learning outcomes may be specific knowledge, skills, and competencies (combinations of skills and knowledge needed for a particular function or activity). Or they may be technical (e.g., ability to use a given software program or technical hardware), work processes (e.g., project management, crisis management), leadership (e.g., style of leadership, treatment of employees, performance management, team building), or interpersonal skills (e.g., communication, negotiation, conflict management). The training may be directed to individuals or intact work groups to improve how the members work together, solve problems, and innovate work methods and/or products or services. Perhaps, more deeply, emotional or sense-making learning that involves worldviews, mind-sets, or introspection can be called upon, improving interpersonal dynamics in the workplace (e.g., diversity and inclusion, civility, breaking stereotypes, overcoming resistance to culture change).

The consultant's role in need analysis is to interpret the client's request and translate objectives into a learning intervention that will bring about desired outcomes. For instance, a prospective client organization may want to contract for the design and implementation of a training program assuming that instructor-led workshops are the solution. The vice president of human resources (HR) may want a leadership training workshop for midlevel managers or a program that introduces a new performance appraisal process. A Chief Operating Officer may want to implement a quality improvement program (e.g., Six Sigma; Keller & Keller, 2010). The VP of marketing may want to implement a new customer relationship management system that the sales staff must learn to use with other sales techniques. Or the information technology department may be launching new business process engineering initiatives to streamline operations or a team approach for software development (e.g., Scrum; Martinelli & Milosevic, 2016). In these cases, who gets trained and the content of training may seem clear. However, learning new methods is one thing; encouraging their use as intended is another. The consultant may have insights about the challenges of transferring the knowledge and skills to the job including the potential for employee resistance to the change.

Employee reactions to work methods may not be evident until the training begins or even until after it is completed. Learning consultants can anticipate challenges and resistance. This may go beyond training to include team discussions about the purpose for a new system, different ways of using it, and the extent to which employees are accountable for its use. Pretraining assessments, interviews, surveys and work sample reviews are all viable avenues to ascertain the challenges that will be faced during learning. The training design itself may need to be molded to improve its effectiveness. The work may be limited to a specific training program, or it may extend to follow-up training or other means of ensuring continuous improvement. Consultants use training or learning paradigms as a foundation for other forms of interventions, for instance, culture change, leadership development, and coaching.

CASE 3.1: NEEDS ANALYSIS AND TRAINING TO INCREASE PROJECT MANAGERS' PRODUCTIVITY

A global consumer products company contracted with a learning consultant for "action learning" (a program that incorporates learning while working on a real problem) to jump-start project teams and make them more effective and efficient (see Marquardt, 2011, for more about action learning). To design a reality-based set of workshops, the consultant asked project team leaders to participate in an online webinar that was highly interactive. The purpose was to give team leaders a voice and to determine their perceptions of the reasons for slow execution. The project managers were located in New York, London, and Singapore. The consultant conducted three online sessions to identify needs and gain buy-in for attendance at subsequent sessions.

Spending time and money on diagnosing the need was worthwhile. By getting clarity on need and identifying realistic problems, the project managers expressed appreciation and offered real-world work challenges, which heightened legitimacy for the subsequent training. Rather than focusing on project management methods (adaptive learning), teams needed training in group dynamics and how to be a high performance team (generative learning).

The consultant worked with the instructional designer and systems developer to construct the team-building workshop with built-in scenarios that challenged participants to handle team problems. The content was based on the problem situations identified in the previous webinars. Videos of simulated project meetings were developed to show leaders and teams dealing with problems associated with *actual* projects in the company. A trainer led group discussions on team dynamics and often polled participants about their ideas for how the scenarios in the videos should play out. Participants could stop the videos whenever they wanted to discuss the perspectives (i.e., needs, expectations, and concerns) of various team members in the videos, suggest the next best action for the project leader, and then continue with the simulation. Short quizzes were embedded so that the consultant could learn what project managers understood and what learning/skills were needed. The participants described the program as "high stakes training with a safety net." Learners were not afraid to suggest courses of action (right or wrong) during the video simulations, and the trainer was skilled at making all choices or tactics in some way reasonable and potentially valuable even if not optimal. Additional training was planned where project managers would bring up global, operational concerns along with team performance concerns. Takeaways from these sessions would become fodder for future training content as well as (if deemed suitable) immediately converted into practice to speed business execution in real time.

STEP 2: CONTRACTING

Understanding and expressing the client's need in the form of a contract is a sound basis for any consultancy. (For excellent sources on contracting for consulting, see Block, 2011; Hattori, 2016; Schein, 2016.) The scope of work should be articulated clearly and be mutually agreed to by all parties. The process of establishing the contract is likely to include one or more meetings, a proposal written by the learning consultant, and discussions with the client to reach agreement on the contract. The contract may specify a more in-depth needs analysis, trial of the training program, and the possibility of using the initial results to fine-tune the program. The contract may be renegotiated if the program's needs analysis and pilot require further work than initially anticipated. The contract should include the time commitment on the part of participants (employees) and resource requirements (facilities, technology, travel, materials). The consultant can also articulate what the client should expect in terms of participants' reactions, behavior change, and bottom-line outcomes (e.g., return on investment in terms of outcomes related to the purpose of the program, perhaps increased sales, increased employee motivation, better communication). Clients need to have realistic expectations, and consultants should be cautious about guaranteeing any bottom-line outcomes. We advise that the consultant and the client obtain legal review of the contract, especially when matters of confidentiality are relevant. Should the work be used to enhance decision-making about personnel (e.g., making job placement decisions based on training results), legal language is often included to address any effect the consultant may have on the employment status of individuals. Additional information related to insurance and other forms of protection may be necessary. The contract will include goals, a timeline, mode(s) of learning delivery (on-the-job, self-paced or classroom based, instructor led, online or in-person), and possibly subcontracting with experts in instructional technology, systems design, or software development. Changes in a contract may be made over time if unexpected events occur. Such possibilities may be phrased generally, since specific events may be hard to anticipate. For instance, the client may suggest midway through a consultancy that the client add employee groups to be trained or expand the program in terms of content and perhaps audience.

The cost of the project can be based on the consultant's per diem or weekly rate, which would allow accounting for any expansion of the program. A clause should deal with payments in the event the client decides to cancel the project for any reason. If the contract specifies a single fee for the scope of work, the consultant needs to estimate the time needed to do the work and allow for possible changes as the work is carried out. Fees will reflect the qualifications of the consultant and very often the nature or complexity of the organizational problem being solved and its value to the business. When the consultant is creating content, the consultant may ask about its use elsewhere or the possibility of licensing it and sharing profits with the client organization, with a sunset rule such that the copyright reverts to the consultant after a period of time.

STEP 3: LEARNING DESIGN AND DEVELOPMENT

Building on the needs analysis, the consultant works with the client organization to design learning methods that are appropriate to the subject matter, the learner, and the organization. Different learning styles fit different elements of the training content. For example, a learning process for a new method for calculating cost overruns in a manufacturing plant may require a statement of principles, a demonstration of application, practice time applied to different scenarios, and testing to determine that students learned the new method. The training can be tailored to the individual learners' abilities. Learners who understand and apply the general principles quickly can move on to more complex cases. Other learners may need more practice time under different scenarios.

Behavioral modeling is a typical approach used to convey inter-personal skills. Behavioral modeling programs, regardless of duration, are likely to include (a) a description of a concept (e.g., conflict resolution, negotiation, improved communication, participative management); (b) step-by-step behaviors; (c) a demonstration of the concept with description, video, and/or role-playing; (d) a time to practice the behaviors with feedback for improvement; and then (e) a time to apply the learned behaviors on the job, with follow-up evaluation by a supervisor or the learning consultant (Taylor, Russ-Eft, & Chan, 2005).

A learning intervention may incorporate one or multiple modes of delivery. Entertainment value is a way to capture attention. This calls for the creative energy of the consultant. The learning consultant can be inventive in creating ways to grab and maintain the learner's attention and reinforce the value of what is learned. Delivery of content is as much an art as it is science. Delivery methods may include lectures in person with time for question and answer or online with videos or podcasts so learners can review the material. In online learning, learners can submit solutions to problems electronically and obtain immediate feedback. They can respond to multiple choice questions, and the software can provide the answers and explanations immediately. (We cover different technologies for training and ongoing learning in Chapter 5.)

The training can provide substantial opportunities to practice new techniques and apply newly acquired knowledge to different situations that parallel those the learner will face on the job. Simulations are especially valuable when the situations to which they apply occur infrequently, such as emergencies and crisis management. Training may also be about what not to do, for instance, teaching participants to avoid demeaning language when speaking with a coworker or customer or ensuring that decisions are not unfair or biased. Put positively, the training may focus on what to do, for example, be respectful and fair, with demonstrations perhaps provided by videos, case studies, and "what if" scenarios for discussion and role-plays. Innovative ways of delivering interactive subject matter include vicarious learning in which actors play a scene and strategically pause for participants to discuss what they are learning. Other similar ways to address highly interactive learning include incorporating skilled actors or assessors who can respond in kind to the behaviors and innuendo of the learners. In such cases, the learning reflects dynamics that happen in the moment. The consultant needs to be experienced in helping participants recognize what they are learning. Highly interactive techniques, including feedback, build experiences that require internalization by the learner so that behavior can change for the better (Diamante, 2009).

Transfer of training requires that simulations be realistic. This does not mean that they have to be exact replicas of work situations. Rather, simulations need face validity or *fidelity*, meaning that learners can picture themselves in the situation and believe that what they are learning has value because it is transferable to their lives at work. For example, a simulation that requires collaborative problem solving to plan how best to close a factory could include examples of on-the-job decisions that give team members a chance to use their knowledge and interpersonal skills.

CASE 3.2: EXAMPLE OF A LEADERSHIP DEVELOPMENT WORKSHOP USING SIMULATION AND BEHAVIOR MODELING

This is an outline of a typical leadership development workshop designed by learning consultants to give participants feedback to guide their learning and experience the demands of higher level responsibility. Participants include high-potential, mid-level managers who are nominated by executives to participate in a leadership development workshop offered by a consulting firm.

Prior to the workshop, participants are asked to complete a 360-degree performance survey online. Participants rate themselves, and they send the survey by e-mail to their supervisor, subordinates, and peers, asking these individuals to rate them. The results will inform the structure of the workshop and are available to the participants at the start of the workshop.

- *Day 1.* The workshop begins with an overview of leadership skills. Most of the day is spent processing the results of the 360-degree performance survey. Workshop staff members who are consulting psychologists meet with each participant individually, reviewing the results and discussing strengths and areas for development.

- *Day 2.* The day begins with a 6-hour business simulation with each participant assuming a different role in the corporation, handling several leadership challenges and decisions. The simulation is followed by time for participants to discuss their behaviors and feelings about their interactions and how they handled the different problems.
- *Day 3.* The theme for the day is transformational leadership. The consultant explains the concept. Participants then role play scenarios, discuss alternative behaviors, receive feedback, and discuss how they can become transformational leaders.
- *Day 4.* The last day consists of time for individual coaching, goal setting, and plans to follow up with the training staff.

Posttraining begins a week after the participants return home. Participants are asked to complete an online evaluation survey. Each participant is assigned to a workshop staff member, who calls every 2 weeks for the next 6 weeks for a 15- to 30-minute telephone coaching session. The 360-degree survey is repeated 6 months after the workshop. Participants receive and discuss the results during an in-person meeting with their coach.

The framework for this type of program was pioneered at the Center for Creative Leadership in Greensboro, North Carolina. For examples of a variety of leader training programs, see the Center's website (https:// www.ccl.org). Numerous training companies and university-based continuing education departments offer such leadership training workshops. An example is the weeklong training program, Leadership and Strategic Impact, offered by The Tuck Executive Education Department at Dartmouth (see http://exec.tuck.dartmouth.edu/programs/open-programs/ leadership-and-strategic-impact). For leadership workshop formats from 2 hours to 2 days, see Russell (2015). For a resource on organizing leadership development workshops from 3 days to 12 weeks in length, see New Leadership Learning Center (2013). For a wide range of approaches to leader development, including those that integrate on-the-job experience with supportive training and coaching, see McCauley and McCall (2014), as well as Van Velsor, McCauley, and Ruderman (2010).

STEP 4: IMPLEMENTATION

A learning intervention does not necessarily go as planned. Suppose attendees did not know what to expect when they attended the training. Suppose supervisors did not know what value their subordinates were supposed to gain from taking time away from their jobs to attend the program. Suppose the participants did not share their learning with their supervisor or coworkers after the training or did not use their newfound knowledge and skills. Suppose the learning conflicted with the department's immediate goals, possibly just because the participants took time away from their work or because the learning did not match current work methods or objectives. Suppose coworkers and supervisors who did not attend the training had little patience for doing things differently based on participants' learning. Learning consultants need to consider how to set the stage for maximum benefit and then evaluate the short- and long-term effects of the training. Hence, Steps 4 and 5.

Implementation can be complicated, time-consuming, and challenging depending on the client and the complexity of the learning intervention. After a training program is designed, tested, and refined, if the consultant is expected to deliver the training, she or he can gain comfort knowing how much time is involved, what to expect from the participants, and how to produce the intended learning outcomes. The program may be customized for the client or may be a program that the consultant developed and customizes for specific clients.

In-person training programs vary in length. They can be a few hours, a day or more, a week, or even a few weeks. The modes of delivery may mix in-person training with electronic and experiential formats (e.g., videos, group discussions, games). The training may be online with the facilitator of learning monitoring use and offering feedback based on participant input or through standardized assessment in the form of test results or other sources of data provided by the client.

Instead of (or in addition to) the learning consultant delivering training, the process may involve training the trainers, for instance, managers or employees who will learn to train others in the organization. The consultant may employ trainers who are subcontractors or employees who can deliver the training under the consultant's oversight. Indeed, learning professionals may themselves be partners in a consulting firm that delivers training services and related consulting. Consulting psychologists can bring tremendous value to the market as experienced professionals with depth in areas such as assessment, counseling, interviewing, consultation, and outcomes measurement coupled with doctoral level understanding and study of human emotion, personality, cognition, and behavior change. Consulting psychologists can contribute to behavioral change using psychoeducational, coaching/counseling, and group-based talk and dialogue (Natale & Diamante, 2005).

STEP 5: ASSESSMENT OF LEARNING OBJECTIVES AND PROGRAM EVALUATION

Just as the client may not immediately appreciate the importance of a needs analysis (Step 1), so too the client may not have the patience for program evaluation. The client may not see the need or be willing to spend the time or money to determine if the intended outcomes materialized. This may seem strange since the client is investing in the training and presumably should want to know the return on the investment. However, the client may assume that the training will be effective and might not invite evidence to the contrary. For example, if the training is in software implementation, the client may take for granted that the participants will learn how to use the software. If the training is related to policy, for instance, online training in tolerance/antibias or managing performance problems such as harassment, the client, likely the HR department, may want all employees to go through the training as soon as possible. The organization may not support a research design that withholds training from one unit to see if the training reduces problems in the unit receiving it. The client may view the learning consultant's role as making sure that the training is based on effective learning principles, so there would be no need for follow-up to see if the program is used as intended or has the desired outcomes.

The consultant may try to convince the client to expand the work to include evaluation. The contract, or a posttraining addendum to it, could use measures of employee satisfaction with the training; tests of learning comprehension and knowledge acquisition; evidence of on-the-job behavior change; and, depending on the purpose of the training, pre-training and posttraining measures of employees' satisfaction, turnover, and performance and, at the unit level, measures of operational efficiency and/or profitability. The evaluation could include a quasi-experimental design that withholds training from some units to compare them with units that received the training, and then later to deliver the training to units that did not receive it earlier. The consultant can use behavior and performance measures as input to improve the relevance and delivery of the subject matter in future training designs (Phillips & Phillips, 2016).

The learning outcomes established in Step 1 are the basis for assessment of learning objectives and program evaluation in Step 5. Measurement of learning may occur as learning progresses within a training program or over time after the program. Measurement during learning can be an opportunity for the consultant to calibrate whether the learning is progressing as intended and enables feedback to the participants that can guide how best to improve learning. This is called *formative* assessment. Measurement at the end of learning is to "grade" the learner—assessing her or his accomplishment and readiness for new assignments, possibly advancement to higher levels of responsibility. This is called *summative* assessment. This may be based on prior research that related performance during or immediately following training to later behaviors, such as job performance in more complex assignments than their positions before training.

What to Measure and When

Measures of learning can include scenarios or problem statements with "What would you do?" multiple choice questions followed by feedback with correct or viable answers and explanations and follow-up questions to be sure learning material has been processed accurately. Measures of learning and online capabilities facilitate adaptive training that progresses in line with the abilities of the participants—with learning materials presented faster for participants who get correct answers and more slowly with additional explanations and demonstrations for participants needing more information and time to digest the concepts and practice new behaviors.

Drawing on Kirkpatrick's (1994; Kirkpatrick & Kirkpatrick, 2006) four-pronged model of learning evaluation, learning outcomes can be (a) reactions to or attitudes about the learning ("Did you like it?," ". . . feel you learned something new?," ". . . believed the trainer was effective?"), (b) demonstrations of new knowledge or skills in tests (recapitulation of information, applications to problem solving, demonstrations of new behaviors), (c) behaviors on the job as evidence of transfer of training, and (d) changes in valued outcomes (measures of job performance). These can be assessed at the individual, team, and organizational levels. Results and feedback may be provided to individual participants. Also, results may be averaged across participants within teams or across teams within the organization as a whole to provide an indication of the program's value. Measures can also reflect team-level activities, such as time spent brainstorming, decision-making method adopted (e.g., voting), use of expertise of individual members, conflict, and conflict resolution. Measures can reflect team-level outcomes such as quality of decisions as indexed by objective measures like the number and quality of units produced in a certain time during a training simulation or game or later on the job. Measures can also assess learning outcomes at the organizational level (e.g., the average attitude and the range of attitudes of employees who participated in the training) as well as organizational level phenomena (e.g., new products, variations on existing products, operational innovations, improvements in return on assets).

The timing of the posttraining assessment on the job is important since intervening factors can affect the trainees' use of what they learned. The sooner after training behaviors and performance are measured, and the more similar the content of the measures are to the content of the training, the more likely the measures are to be the result of the training. The more distant the measure is from the training in time and content, the more the measurement results are likely to be affected by variables in the environment other than the training. A sound strategy is to collect multiple measures at various time intervals, including participants' reactions to the training, performance tests immediately following training, behaviors on the job that show whether trainees can apply what they learned, and ongoing job performance measures at the individual and unit or organization level.

The first training case above, the 4-day leader development program, can serve as an example. Participants can be asked how they felt about each element of the training (e.g., 360-degree feedback, coaching, leadership styles lecture and demonstrations). The participants' performance in the behavioral exercise that were the basis for the assessor to give them feedback and coaching could be reported. The evaluations made by the assessors at the end of the training used to make decisions about the participants could also be reported. Measures can be collected 3 to 6 months after training, for instance, a repeat of the presurvey with coworkers evaluating the participants' leadership style and effectiveness. Measures of the participants' leadership outcomes may include data on departmental productivity (e.g., units produced, dollars earned).

Control and Comparison Groups

The goal of a research design is to attribute the results to the learning intervention rather than to other factors that may affect the results. Program evaluation needs to eliminate as well as possible alternative explanations for the results other than the training. Conditions are difficult to control, but steps can be taken to minimize confounds in the results. For example, participants who are trained can be compared to a similar group of participants who did not receive training, at least not yet (these are *control* groups). Other *comparison* groups may receive different varieties of the training to determine which training components are most valuable, perhaps comparing alternative learning programs (e.g., contrasting in-person, classroom-delivered training to on-the-job, self-paced learning). The comparison and control groups will not be identical to the training group, but they can be structured to be as similar as possible, for instance, in mix of age, gender, experience, and education. All groups would receive the same pre- and postmeasures and be tracked for the same amount of time. However, external factors may still influence the results, for instance, if by chance, many members of the control group were affected by some event that did not affect as many members of the trained group. A comparison of results would suggest that the training was highly effective, but this would be an erroneous conclusion. So the learning consultant needs to take into account the context of the training and conditions in the environment over time that may affect the measures.

Alternative research designs can produce valuable results with fewer resources, although with more limitations on the precision of the conclusions. For example, the control group participants can receive training later so that all employees eventually have a chance to benefit from the training. However, this may eliminate being able to make conclusive statements about the long-term outcomes of the training. Another strategy may be to train everyone but have more measures before and after the training so that changes in behaviors and outcome that emerge immediately after training and persist can be attributed to the training and not to other factors.

Measurement and research design are even more challenging when the goal is to create a team that is innovative or an organization that is adept at adjusting to changing conditions (i.e., has moved toward becoming a learning organization; Senge et al., 2014). One training program will likely not be sufficient to instill sustainable learning habits. This may require teams to experience challenges and process how they applied what they learned in a training program and, perhaps more important, what they learned from working through a challenge or problem as part of a structured learning experience. In fact, much of the learning that will affect team-level performance might require introspection, a rather private, individualized event. For instance, creativity is unleashed when ego is not a personal factor and evaluation is not part of the equation (Kilmann, 1994).

The learning consultant can facilitate discussions about learning in ways that help team members be mindful of what they learned and how they learn. These discussions can be incorporated into the program evaluation, and they can be summarized and reported to the client to show value and also pinpoint gaps for future development within teams and for the organization as a whole. In addition, the consultant might choose to engage learners privately and confidentially to access thoughts and emotions before and after training, summarizing the findings across participants and then sharing them with the group. This can be a valuable springboard for additional inquiry about the training while also serving as a stimulus for self-discovery. Such methods turn the evaluation process into yet another learning event.

Learning Reports

In addition to evaluating a specific training program, the organization's chief learning or HR officer may prepare an annual learning and development report about learning across the organization as a whole or units within the organization. The officer may hire a learning consultant to advise about the content, collection, and presentation of data. The report can include three sections: (a) *basic data* (e.g., hours spent on training, number of programs delivered, training cost per employee, ratio of learning and development budget to total HR budget), (b) *online learning* (e.g., percentage of all formal learning that was delivered online, percentage of hours trained online, percentage of employees with access to online training content, percentage of employees who started and percentage who completed online content, and cost avoidance due to reduced travel, venue, and employee time away), and (c) *efficiency* (e.g., time to learn, time to competence including on the job practice and application, and cost per training hour; CrossKnowledge, 2016).

Calculating Return on Investment (ROI) in Learning

Some clients view training as an expense. This implies that the training is part of the cost of operations but does not add value. However, training should be viewed as an investment in HR that adds value to the enterprise and has a bottom-line impact. It is fair and reasonable to state the value-added of learning and development to the enterprise. Here's how: ROI (%) = (Benefit – Cost)/Cost.

The cost of training is the dollar value of the improvement in outputs. Outputs might be reduced employee turnover, fewer errors needing correction, more units produced in a given period of time, increases in efficiency (time for production), increases in quality (fewer returned units), and less time wasted (e.g., spent on interpersonal conflicts; Kaminski & Lopes, 2009). There may be several benefits, and their value can be added. The benefits require comparing change from pre- to posttraining minus the changes that might have occurred without the training, for example, due to spending the time gaining more experience. The cost includes the learning consultant's time, cost of materials and facilities, and cost of employees' time such as pay and reduced productivity during that time.

Here is an example of an evaluation of training in quality management. Say there are two similar business units in one company. One unit participates in team training focused on quality improvement, the other does not. The teams that participated in the training showed a 20% improvement in work output from pre- to posttraining. The teams that did not participate in the training showed a 5% improvement over the same time period. This suggests that the training improved output by 15% beyond what might have occurred without the training. This can be translated into a dollar value of the improved output. The cost of training can be calculated by the cost of the consultant and the hourly rate of the employees who participated in the training. The cost is subtracted from the benefit and the difference is divided by the cost to show the benefit as a proportion of the cost (Pyzdek & Keller, 2014).

If a 15% improvement is worth $55,000 per team per year and the cost of the training was $15,000, then the ROI was more than two and a half (2.67 to be exact) times the cost—not a bad return! Presumably, the added value would continue over time. The extent to which the results are sustained or diminished can also be calculated to determine the long-term impact of the training. The productivity gain may be short-lived if the productivity of the teams that did not receive training (the control group) catches up to the productivity of the group that received training after, say, 1 year. Still, the training produced a worthwhile return for the teams that received it, suggesting that all teams should be trained. The consultant discovering this result could suggest that additional training may increase the value further or offer other ways to speed execution of training and perhaps broaden impact across the organization.

CASE 3.3: EXAMPLE OF EVALUATIONS GUIDING A SEQUENTIAL "LEADERSHIP FOR INNOVATION" LEARNING INTERVENTION

Assessment can be both a foundation (needs analysis) and a guide for learning. A $500 million nutrition products company found itself facing emerging threats from much larger, multinational pharmaceutical companies. Essentially, the stronghold the company once enjoyed in the domestic market began to loosen. Larger, very aggressive pharmaceutical companies identified this "nutriceutical" market as a growth industry, and they wanted in. The smaller nutrition company realized that it needed to take action to hold onto market share. The CEO hired a consulting psychologist to help top brand managers to recognize the competition and stimulate their teams to be more innovative.

To begin the "leadership for innovation" development program, the consultant administered a series of measures to assess characteristics of the managers that may be barriers to change (an example of Step 1: Needs Analysis). The consultant discovered that as a group, the brand managers were low on openness to experience, high on goal orientation (a focus on meeting objectives rather than learning), and high on dominance. The consultant negotiated a contract to deliver a 1-day training workshop for the managers starting with a report of these results and discussions on how these characteristics could be barriers to leading innovation (Step 2: Contracting and Step 3: Design). The managers agreed quickly that they were reluctant to explore new ideas and try novel approaches that might cause them to miss performance targets. The participants ended the day with a discussion of what they could do lead their teams to be more innovative. Each of the managers needed to become an agent of change.

The consultant then developed a second training intervention (a new contract for a more extensive design): an online slide tutorial on leading innovation. Implementation (Step 4) included leading teams in strategies such as obtaining data about competitors, conducting focus groups with customers, analyzing data from customers who ordered products online, conducting brainstorming meetings, and using social media marketing. Questions were embedded throughout the slides. The session took managers about 2 hours to complete. The last slide included a link to a quiz (Step 5: Evaluation) to be sure the managers understood the concepts. Some managers complained to the consultant that they didn't have 2 hours to spend in front of the computer reading slides. Another complaint was that the material described principles for action that did not recognize the difficulty in implementing them. They needed more hands-on experiences in leading innovation.

During the next phase, about 3 weeks after most of the managers completed the online tutorial (the consultant had to cajole a few of the managers to complete it), the organization negotiated a contract for the consultant to bring the managers together again for a second day of training, this time to participate in an action learning challenge. Each manager was assigned an initiative that focused on an aspect of leading innovation, such as reducing fixed costs, monitoring the competition, and accelerating new product commercialization. The participants shared their ideas and gave each other constructive comments and suggestions.

Six months after the training, the consultant recommended, and the organization agreed, to a contract that specified the consultant develop and administer a company-wide survey of employee engagement (a more extensive assessment). Items in the survey, measured on a 5-point Likert scale, included evaluation of the goals of the leadership development interventions with items such as "I feel a part of change," "Innovation is a top priority," and "We're moving forward to beat the competition." The results were fed back to the managers during a subsequent workshop. The consultant presented the survey results, which showed that higher performing team leaders had become more open and had implemented innovation strategies to a greater extent than the lower performing team leaders. The participants then discussed the results and their leadership strategies. The participants were keenly aware that their bonuses depended on their performance, which, undoubtedly, played a motivational role. After the learning consultants shared the results of the company-wide survey with the participants, the company—in collaboration with the learning consultant—made plans to coach executives as ambassadors of innovation.

After the company-survey results were reviewed, the consultant helped to hire a group of external coaches to work with the team leaders. The consultant developed methods for the coaches to use, including individual assessments (based on Big Five personality factors), multisource data (i.e., feedback surveys from peers, direct reports, and supervisors), and a custom protocol that connected survey results to individual assessment, which helped team leaders think about how their characteristics and behavior affected how others see them, and how they could improve the performance of their team.

The case shows a comprehensive and long-term approach to organization change. The learning consultant used data to demonstrate the need for change and the value of learning interventions.

CONCLUSION

This chapter examined five basic steps consultants follow to develop a learning intervention (needs analysis, contracting, design, implementation, and evaluation). We showed how needs analysis shapes a learning intervention in relation to discoveries of the "real" needs that the organization should address. Needs and expectations are reflected in the contract that the consultant establishes with the client. Case 3.1 showed the evolution of a learning intervention as the learning consultant obtained input from employees and developed interactive methods that broadened learning from a focus on tasks to a focus on team and organizational processes. Design and implementation followed. Case 3.2 described a leadership training program that uses a variety of components, including simulations and behavior modeling. We recommended building in evaluation—including reactions to the learning, demonstrations of learning, behavior changes, and application on the job (transfer of learning). Evaluations in beta tests of a training program can suggest ways to fine-tune methods and improve outcomes. However, rigorous assessments are not always possible, and learning consultants should recognize the extent to which limited assessments have value for clients and learners. Case 3.3 showed how assessments evaluated and guided the leader training. The case showed that learning consultants occasionally encounter uncooperative individuals or teams—maybe even an entire organization. The consultant can encourage cooperation by explaining the need for participation and using evaluation results to demonstrate success and reinforce the learning. We build on the notions of creating individual, team, and organizational change through learning interventions in Chapter 4, and we explore ways to support adaptive, generative, and transformative learning.

4

Designing Learning Interventions for Facilitating Adaptive, Generative, and Transformative Learning

A useful distinction for the consultant developing training programs is the difference between adaptive, generative, and transformative learning (see the definitions in the Introduction). Each serves a different need and accomplishes different goals for a client organization. Each can apply at the level of individual employees, teams, and the organization as a whole. In this chapter and in Chapter 5, we strive to understand the shift from instructor-controlled adaptive learning to learner-driven generative learning, with particular attention to unlocking the value of new technologies for training and development.

Training has been shown to reduce errors in a wide range of high risk occupations, such as emergency rooms, aviation, and the military as well

http://dx.doi.org/10.1037/0000094-005
Learning Interventions for Consultants: Building the Talent That Drives Business, by M. London and T. Diamante

as conventional organizations (Salas et al., 2012). Investing in employees helps the organization remain competitive and is a valuable means of attracting talent to the organization and retaining them. However, the wrong training can be dysfunctional, just as the right training can produce positive results. Obviously, training that is improperly designed, delivered, and implemented can be costly and ineffective.

Learning objectives may be fairly straightforward, especially when the skills and knowledge to be learned and expectations for job performance are clear. However, more often than not, learning goals and behavioral expectations are not all that clear. Applications depend on circumstances (e.g., demands, uncertainties, and ambiguities in a sea of complexity and even chaos). Some learning is adaptive—incremental knowledge and skills that improve behavior. Other learning is generative—more developmental, arising from job experiences, training, and coaching. Learning can also be transformative, with dramatic shifts in how work is done to meet changing goals or for discovering new ways of working as a consequence of exploration, curiosity, and observation.

Learning design should follow needs analysis and learning objectives. The objectives may be clear and straightforward. This is the case with adaptive learning. The training may be a single event (in-person or online workshops or presentations) or a series of events over time on such topics as finance, marketing, operations, and human resources (HR) management. Another topic might be business acumen aimed at helping managers to understand the contribution they make to the company's stock price. Other topics might be leadership, economic prospects in the region and industry, new technologies, project management, and diversity, inclusion, and equal treatment in the workforce. A workshop might last anywhere from an hour a week in a webinar format to a multiday course meeting once a week during a period of a month or more, or an intensive week-long course, perhaps off-site. Duration will depend on such factors as the complexity of the material, the immediacy of need, the resources available, and the availability of the participants. The programs may draw participants from different company locations.

GUIDELINES FOR TRAINING DESIGN

Consider the following guidelines for making training valuable for learners and the organization (Chen & Klimoski, 2007; Salas et al., 2012). First, conduct a training needs analysis (e.g., analyses of job requirements, the organization's needs for skills and knowledge, and individual employees' abilities and motivation). Prepare the learning climate. This includes scheduling training when employees are available and can be spared from the job. Prepare supervisors and leaders so they will understand the purpose of the training and the value it will provide to their units. This is key, so that participants are supported for their learning efforts when not in the training. Implement policy or communications to demonstrate organizational value for the training initiative. During training, encourage a positive mind-set in trainees. Let them experience, through practice and results, that they are capable of learning. Reward them for wanting to learn more. Follow learning principles (e.g., opportunities to observe, practice, receive feedback to learn from their errors, and improve). Use technology wisely by structuring user control and use simulations to enhance learning. (We cover learning technologies in Chapter 5.) After training, help learners apply their new knowledge and skills (transfer of training). Remove obstacles to transfer: make sure they have opportunities to use newly learned knowledge and skills and the information, resources, and/or time necessary to utilize acquired skills. Evaluate training and communicate the value to the learners, supervisors, and leadership. Capitalize on the evaluation results to improve future training.

TRAINING DESIGN FOR ADAPTIVE, GENERATIVE, AND TRANSFORMATIVE LEARNING

London and Hall (2011) outlined how training design and implementation vary for adaptive, generative, and transformative learning. *Adaptive learning* is delivered through technology or an instructor, perhaps with opportunities to practice, receive feedback, and improve. Learning consultants move through the process of giving step-by-step instructions (concrete experience) that learners should understand and be ready to apply in the same way (reflective observation). Convergent thinking gives rise to deductive reasoning, applying the rules to different conditions (abstract reasoning). Consultants give learners a chance to practice under controlled conditions, applying the rules to a range of problems and receiving feedback until the learners "get it right" (active exploration).

Generative learning is self-paced, with employees as individuals or teams using multiple methods facilitated by trainers and consultants. The trainer is the "sage on the stage" for adaptive learning, the "guide on the side" for generative learning. Learning consultants initiate a discussion with learners about problems that do not lend themselves to fixed rules (concrete experience). Consultants facilitate divergent thinking through discussions about the elements of problems, brainstorming with learners to recognize possible alternative causes and solutions (reflective observation), and using inductive reasoning by actively questioning (abstract conceptualization) and testing assumptions through trial-and-error experiments to create new modes of operating (active exploration).

Transformative learning brings about individual, team, and organizational change in response to changing conditions or as strategic initiatives to get ahead of the competition. Transformative learning responds to the rapid pace of change in organizations as new business models appear rapidly. Organizations are changing how they behave and so the behavior inside the organization requires change as well (Salas et al., 2012). Consultants engage with learners in messy, even chaotic, situations. In a world of relentless, constant change, we might call for learners who thrive in chaotic situations (concrete experience). Their impromptu, unplanned, and unanticipated insights may allow them to imagine what no one else has yet conceived. Consultants coach learners through convergent and divergent thinking in ways that synthesize input and ultimately formulate novel designs and problem solutions (reflective observation). Consultants encourage inductive and deductive reasoning, dynamic thought processes, and discussions (abstract conceptualization) that stimulate active exploration of new behaviors and work processes (active exploration).

Training goals and methods are likely to be an amalgam of adaptive, generative, and transformative learning to different degrees. Consider the following examples of mainly adaptive learning:

- communicating policies across an organization for risk management and HR policy;
- addressing problems of discrimination, preventing harassment and microaggression, promoting diversity and gender equity;
- satisfying federal court orders;
- communicating ethics and integrity expectations;
- conducting new employee orientation; and
- determining the role and value of required program participation for introducing policy changes.

These are examples of adaptive learning in that they are areas the organization should or must implement for good business practice and possibly compliance with government regulations and laws. Employees should be aware of these policies and procedures and are likely to be responsible for implementing them. These may improve the organization's performance and efficiency and be integrated into the organization's culture.

Examples that combine adaptive and generative learning include

- instituting new ways of working, such as telecommuting geographically dispersed teams bridging language, cultures, and time zones;
- implementing new performance management programs, for instance, processes for selection, orientation, appraisal (formal and ongoing), feedback, and/or employee development; and
- facilitating peer-to-peer learning through coaching and mentoring programs, for example, HR and organization strategy interventions, top team meetings, and executive coaching programs as a start to cascading goals, policies, and cultural dimensions throughout the organization.

Some of these activities may be new to the organization. The organization adapts to changing conditions and goes further to improve working relationships and operations, and in that sense, their implementation becomes generative (i.e., new for the organization and possibly an innovative way of complying with regulations or instituting new leadership strategies).

Examples that combine generative and transformative learning include

- shifting organizational strategy—such as shifting from a domestic to an international focus, growing beyond a narrow niche, or supporting a multicultural workforce;
- learning to get things done in team settings;
- embedding new business processes using organizational strategy and learning processes (i.e., enabling the organization to do new things while also learning how to do new things better, simulating business operations for the sake of efficiency analysis and enhancement);
- stimulating organization change, such as empowering teams to solve problems and be innovative;
- identifying and promoting high-potential individuals as leaders, change agents, and impact champions;
- advancing women as experts and leaders in STEM fields, including medicine;
- evaluating options for leadership development;
- forecasting learning needs relative to data about employees' skills, knowledge, and base of experience; and
- brainstorming and implementing innovations in response to new technology and the growth of a new competitor.

These examples are generative in that they are new to the organization. They also transform the organization in novel innovative directions that become the cutting edge of best practice. In the process, employees and managers learn not only to adapt but also to generate new and better methods of operating, and to transform the organization and themselves to be successful in different ways than they were. Generative and, especially, transformative learning programs engage employees through innovation, and they provide avenues to have a positive impact on customers, suppliers, and other stakeholders.

CASE 4.1: ADAPTIVE LEARNING

Implementing new policies and procedures for cybersecurity in an organization provides an example of adaptive learning. Implementation steps included educating employees about the importance of guarding and frequently changing passwords, not using private social media and web browsing on the job, avoiding e-mails from unknown senders, and other precautions. A learning consultant developed an online multimedia presentation to explain the policies and procedures. The presentation, which was mandatory for all employees, included slides and videos about the new procedures, measures the information technology (IT) department had taken to install firewalls, an introduction to how the employer deployed software to identify potential risk (internally and/or externally driven), recommendations to go beyond the policies to safeguard data and systems, and an invitation to use the online suggestion box for employees to share experiences and submit ideas. To apply Kolb's (1981) theory, the training included rules to follow and case examples of how to apply them in standard and more unusual situations. In learning programs such as this, consultants may also consider using simulations, conducting question and answer sessions, and offering resources to handle any follow-up questions or address additional, unaddressed needs. In this case, supervisors were given a guideline to provide on-the-job follow-up training to ensure employees were following the new procedures.

CASE 4.2: GENERATIVE LEARNING

Consider the support a learning consultant provided for advancing women as experts and leaders in a successful investment firm where only 8% of senior investment officers and analysts were women. The HR staff were working on recruiting more experienced women and hiring recent graduates into entry level positions with the goal of building a pipeline of women who aspire to leadership positions. However, the CEO and HR vice president recognized that this required more than a new policy and recruitment. It meant a concerted effort at culture change to welcome and mentor women in an environment of openness and collegiality—more of a generative than an adaptive change.

The learning consultant began by holding focus groups with the senior women in the firm about their perceptions of the challenges for women in this organization and the industry in general. Participants responded after the consultant assured them of confidentiality. The consultant used summaries of the focus groups as input for discussions with the senior team and repeated the discussions with groups of mid- to higher level managers below the vice president level. The consultant developed case examples for the managers to review. The goal was for the groups to identify proactive measures they could take to recognize the challenges women face, and for male managers to understand that they were giving patronizing feedback and imposing differential standards, for instance, low evaluations of women who were viewed as counternormative (e.g., aggressive, like the men, but not meek and nurturing as the men expected). To apply Kolb's theory, this was a problem for which organization members did not have a clear understanding or a clear path to change. The work and career experience was different for men and women. The consultant facilitated divergent thinking through discussions about the problem from multiple perspectives. The consultant facilitated active questioning in discussions and private conversations with individual executives and managers. They needed to test their assumptions through the case work and develop goals, implementation strategies, and plans for follow-up. The need for heightened interpersonal sensitivity during engagement with the client was noteworthy.

CASE 4.3: TRANSFORMATIVE LEARNING

A learning consultant worked with a business unit that transitioned from selling computer products to providing consulting services for improved efficiency in client companies. Employees wondered about their job security in the face of different skill requirements, about how quickly the firm planned to make the change, and about differences in compensation. The business unit needed a new organizational structure, new job descriptions, and most important, the commitment of employees to making the change successfully. Applying Kolb's approach, the learning consultant led in person workshops to discuss what the new work goals and jobs meant and how employees could develop their skills in what seemed to them to be a chaotic situation. They needed to see how other companies accomplished similar changes. Also, since there were no set patterns of work, employees could formulate their own designs and solutions to anticipated problems. The consultant encouraged brainstorming and experimentation by (a) having employees interview current and prospective service clients about their expectations in the competitive technology service market; (b) creating ways the business unit might address client expectations and identify new ideas for surprising clients in ways that surpass the competition; (c) experimenting, evaluating, and refining these new work processes over time; and (d) through a series of sessions, addressing employees' uncertainties and confidence. The process recognized employees' passion for the work and that not all current employees would want, or have the needed skills, to stay with the company.

Guidelines for Adaptive, Generative, and Transformative Learning

In summary, the following are guidelines for applying different learning methods for adaptive, generative, and transformative learning.

- Use adaptive, instructor-provided learning for delivery of concrete material that is linear and cumulative. This would include standard procedures that need to be followed in a particular work operation.
- Use generative learning designs for problem solving and learner exploration, conceptualization, and reflection. Open-ended exploration allows discussion to analyze problems, generate alternative possible solutions, try some, implement a course of action, evaluate results, and fine-tune the action strategies.
- Use adaptive and generative learning designs together to stimulate transformative learning that encompasses learning new standard procedures and applying them in unanticipated ways to meet uncertain

and sometimes chaotic situations. Problem analysis is critical, but so is facing the dynamic (rapidly changing) environment that presents new and unique challenges requiring input from diverse sources. Acquiring new skills and knowledge and, more generally, learning how to deal with unanticipated change are valuable skills for individual, team, and organizational transformation.

Designs for generative and transformative learning are likely to combine methods over time, such as the following:

- a comprehensive leadership development program that gives participants feedback and coaching, as well as a chance to take part in simulations;
- a product quality improvement program that involves examining and brainstorming ways to improve work processes while learning about team building and innovation creation techniques;
- an organizational change intervention—for instance, a merger with an international firm could require learning about the new firm as well as learning about characteristics of the countries in which the newly combined firm will operate along with cultural sensitivity training (information about and time to practice the norms in different cultures) and facilitated discussions about restructuring jobs, reporting relationships, and stress management; and
- a new enterprise-wide software system that changes work processes and requires learning new applications while maintaining current productivity.

IMPLICATIONS OF LEARNING ORIENTATION FOR INTERVENTION DESIGN

Learning theories address different ways that individuals learn, and suggest that some people learn best in particular ways. Building on Knowles's (1984) concept of adult learners as being self-motivated and self-paced, some individuals are *expansive* learners with a *mastery learning orientation*. They are ready and eager to learn and seek new learning opportunities and continuous self-improvement, and they are high in self-monitoring, self-efficacy, and self-regulation (Diamante & London, 2002; Dweck, 1986; London & Diamante, 2002). They require a different level of support and encouragement than individuals who are low on these constructs, who do not take learning into their own hands, and want to be told what to do. Expansive learners are ripe for generative and transformative learning experiences. They are quick learners when it comes to adaptive learning. They absorb new rules, regulations, standards, knowledge, and skills quickly and then find novel ways to apply them. In contrast to mastery learners, *performance learners* aim to achieve immediate performance goals and avoid failures. They respond to step-by-step education and they want to follow the steps precisely and apply them in a regimented manner to find the right solution.

The learning facilitator needs to recognize that people vary in their readiness for adaptive, generative, and transformative learning. Adaptive learning programs appeal to performance learners, and mastery learners also need to acquire the same knowledge. Adaptive learning programs convey concepts, demonstrate them, give participants a chance to practice them, and then expect participants to apply the concepts on the job. Mastery learners may approach the learning as an opportunity to expand on the concepts conveyed in the training, perhaps applying them in new ways. But the goal for all participants is to acquire and apply the knowledge.

Training professionals may need to assess the individuals as they start the learning process, or even as they are selected for learning. Consultants can ask questions of supervisors who are selecting participants, or they can ask volunteers about their learning experiences or approaches to learning. They will identify mastery learners—people who strive constantly to learn and improve, develop new skills, acquire new knowledge, and seek challenges and are likely to thrive in generative and transformative learning experiences (Grant & Dweck, 2003). Performance learners will be able to contribute in these environments, perhaps helping to transfer novel ideas to concrete operations.

Learning orientation applies to teams as well as individuals. At the team level, members learn to interact, try new routines, break out of old habits, receive feedback, change membership, orient new members, and ultimately, become learning units or organizations that can quickly address change when needed or create change to improve organizational outcomes. London and Sessa (2006, 2007) developed a model of learning that applies to teams. The model proposes that stimuli provide pressures to learn. Stimuli may be external forces or internal motivation. The state of a team's "readiness to learn" includes a willingness to go beyond current boundaries in order to do things differently. Adaptive team learning processes are reactive forms of coping, using current capabilities to manage pressures. Generative team learning processes are proactive and purposeful, encouraging team members to experiment with new skills; explore alternative methods; observe other teams; and identify, modify, and adopt best practices. Transformative team learning is radical re-creation that can entail, for example, giving up old interaction patterns, creating new modes of operation, members reflecting on the team's success, evaluating ideas by experimentation, and choosing new modes of operation based on results.

Overall, whether for adaptive, generative, or transformative individual or team learning for performance or mastery learners, (a) the learning environment and delivery must be pleasant (or at least, not aversive); (b) the learned material must be delivered clearly and in relation to the learners' cognitive abilities (complex information that is presented quickly will not be internalized); and (c) the learners must be motivated to learn and have an opportunity to use the learning after training without other events or ancillary learned material interfering, including material that was used previously and ingrained in memory, as old routine behaviors would be. Performance learners will be open to adaptive changes and integrate them quickly. Mastery learners will be active participants in generative changes that contribute to their own development as well as that of the team or organization. They will thrive on opportunities for transformative change and indeed will initiate it when the opportunity arises, suggesting and experimenting with novel ideas. Several companies promote intrapreneurship by giving employees time to work on their own ideas and create their own projects (3M's "skunk works" and Google's "20% time"), although this presents the challenge of having sufficient time to do their main jobs—a challenge that is not likely to hamper mastery learners. (For companies that promote intrapreneurship, see https://www.vocoli.com/blog/may-2014/10-inspiring-examples-of-successful-intrapreneurship; for "the truth" about whether Google employees have time for personal projects, see http://www.businessinsider.com/google-20-percent-time-policy-2015-4.)

Action Learning

In reviewing learning theory in Chapter 2, we focused on the value of experiential learning, especially for generative and transformative learning, which we discussed earlier in this chapter and defined in Chapter 1. This draws on the concept of *action learning* (Revans, 2011). Action learning (also called *experiential learning*) involves small groups working on real problems, taking action, and learning in the process of taking action as individuals, as a team, and/or as an organization. It helps organizations develop creative, flexible, and successful strategies to pressing problems. Action learning is a way to teach underlying principles and methods in contexts that are meaningful to the learner. Learning can be combined with solving real problems that the organization faces, such as introducing a new product or service or seeking ways to increase efficiency or improve communication. For example, a warehouse distribution team may practice principles of leadership and team cooperation, as well as logistics, by designing ways to solve a societal problem, such as the distribution of medication to war-torn or remote areas using drones. As the learning unfolds, the learners can see how it will improve their performance and that of the unit.

Consultants can design active, agentic (self-controlled) learning, which is important when learners need to take action (Bandura, 2001; Biesta & Tedder, 2007). Entrepreneurship is an example—particularly applying entrepreneurial skills to solve difficult problems, such as poverty in developing countries. Frese, Gielnik, and Mensmann (2016) reported on a 2- to 3-day action-regulation workshop that focused on self-regulation and active behavior to enhance each learner's personal initiative as an entrepreneur in a developing country. Learning centered on how to show personal initiative in setting goals, searching for information and opportunities, planning actions and executing them, and seeking feedback to detect problems with their approach. For each element of their initiative, participants focused on immediate issues, a long-term orientation, and persistence. The entrepreneurs were asked to identify trends in the market and set goals that were different from competitors to address immediate issues. They were also asked to generate ideas for meeting what they anticipated might be future market needs (long-term perspective). They were encouraged not to be discouraged when barriers emerge (persistence). In monitoring and seeking feedback, they might ask former customers why they stopped buying a product or ask stakeholders what they perceive to be their biggest challenges and opportunities, seeking input from a wide variety of sources (Frese et al., 2016; Glaub & Frese, 2011). For transfer of knowledge, learners actively practiced what they learned and received feedback while starting a personal initiative in their firm, such as introducing new products or services or using unconventional marketing techniques. In addition to the workshop's value for NGOs and existing entrepreneurs in developing countries, the workshop could be implemented in any organization that has corporate social responsibility as part of its mission.

In summary, consultants can create action learning opportunities by having individuals and teams address actual problems, explore why the problems occurred, design and implement ways to overcome them, evaluate their success, participate in their continued improvement, and discuss and recognize what they learned along the way.

CASE 4.4: ACTION LEARNING FOR CHANGE AND INNOVATION

Learning interventions can be adaptive, generative, and/or transformational in design. Adaptive learning interventions may use current, identifiable situations to which learners can easily apply new methods for improved performance. Examples might be using a new database for filing and retrieving customer information. Training for generative learning may give employees a chance to apply the new database to other work problems, perhaps combining the database with analytic software that reports frequency of different types of customer interactions and suggests actions for improved customer relationships. Transformational learning interventions may engage customers by giving them access to the database plus an analytic tool, so that they identify their own needs. The learning consultant may be the architect of a creative, disruptive way to educate employees and build better work processes as a result.

The following is an example of a workshop intended to stimulate innovative solutions to problems. This example is based on techniques developed at General Electric. Behavioral modeling was developed during the 1970s, and "Work Out" was developed during the 1980s (Ulrich, Kerr, & Ashkenas, 2002) and adapted currently in Six Sigma quality improvement processes.

- *Participants.* Four product management teams (consisting of four or five managers each) were invited to participate in a customized training for a consumer products company. Each team represented a product manufactured and sold by the company. Multiple sessions with different participants were held during a 2-year period.
- *Day 1.* The trainer presented concepts on team innovation, brainstorming methods and psychological dimensions that can make or break creativity, with examples of teams that created innovations to produce improved product designs with input from customers, and drawing on the diverse expertise in the team of product designers, engineers, supply chain coordinators, and brand managers. Participants discussed the examples throughout the day and considered their relevance to their own organization.
- *Day 2.* Participants were organized into new groups with no more than one other person with whom they worked on the job. A senior executive in the firm presented a challenge or problem to solve for the company (e.g., open new markets in Asia, beat a competitor's prices, create a new supply chain, design a new inventory tracking system). As the group members worked, trainers observed the group and took notes on leadership emergence, knowledge sharing, and styles of communication and task-oriented teamwork (e.g., showing patience, expressing

ideas, evaluating others' ideas critically or constructively, being aggressive, initiating direction). The day ended with planning for subsequent work before the next session.

- *Intervening 4 weeks.* Participants returned to their work settings. During this period, they communicated with workshop group members to continue working on the challenge. Those who were not colocated interacted by online meetings while posting and working on documents on cloud-based software.

- *Day 3.* Participants returned to the training site to finalize and present their work to the senior executive. The executive provided feedback. Then the groups had time to discuss the results and to process what had worked well and what had not in their group work during the intervening 4 weeks.

- *Day 4.* Participants disbanded their training group and met with participants with whom they worked on the job to discuss what they had learned about themselves and teamwork and consider how they could apply the learning to their own team. The experience in the training groups provided a fresh perspective as well as time to get to know others in the organization, which was intended to help communication across teams and suggest new ways for collaboration.

  The manager of each team then presented a project for the team to work on during the next 2 weeks. Although the members of the team worked together regularly, this assignment presented a challenge to focus on their working relationship and apply what they learned about team interaction to their own team's effectiveness.

- *Intervening 2 weeks.* As team members conducted their usual work, they met and worked individually on the assigned project.

- *Day 5.* The teams met again at the training site. Each team presented work on their project. Then team members had time to discuss their team process and present what they learned to the larger group—how they applied what they learned during the earlier mixed-group challenge and how this affected work in their homework team. Team members also discussed how the earlier experience would help them in the future as they are assigned to projects, becoming members of new teams for short duration projects to develop rapid, lasting improvements in products and work methods, and then returning to their home team where they could do the same in a mode of continuous improvement.

The trainers shared notes, provided feedback and coaching to the teams, identified and dealt with positive and negative dynamics vis-à-vis innovation, and followed up with the teams by assessing changes in behavior and outcomes.

CASE 4.5: LEARNING BASED ON SURVEY FEEDBACK AND LEARNING READINESS PLANS

To enhance workforce engagement, a learning facilitator was contracted to create and administer an employee attitude survey with the employees (1,000 in all) of the U.S. offices of an international medical technology company. The engagement survey measured (a) leadership credibility, (b) communication, (c) work–life satisfaction, (d) motivation for the work itself/engagement, (e) satisfaction with management, (f) opportunities for learning and development, and (g) global mobility. Results were compared for all departments. The senior managers of those departments in the bottom quartile were gathered for an engagement day delivered by the learning facilitator. The day, however, was disengaging if not disheartening. The bottom quartile was not a good place to be and, though unsaid, these managers worried not only about the data but also about competing with their fellow managers and saving their own careers.

The C-suite of vice presidents wanted the bottom layer of management improved, and they viewed use of the survey as a constant motivator for managers to "wake up and worry about the next round of surveys!" This might not seem like the most supportive or kind organizational culture. In fairness, though, business was not good. There was a sense that management had grown complacent and large, so inadequate performance was being identified and fixed.

The consultant was next asked to prepare a series of workshops for seven senior managers whose business units needed to be improved. The assessments measured (a) managerial capability, (b) leadership potential,

(c) openness to criticism, (d) conscientiousness, (e) business-based decision making (planning, prioritizing, delegating, and management), and (f) emotional intelligence (self-monitoring, interpersonal judgment, emotion regulation, and organizational acumen).

The assessments were administered individually by the consultant to each of the managers. The assessments included standardized personality assessment, a structured interview (behaviorally based and situational), business cases (requiring written responses), and a 360-degree assessment and review of their performance record (i.e., evaluation). These data were converted into a *learning readiness plan*—a document that essentially summarized each manager's strengths and challenges relative to the negative data points on the engagement survey. When coworkers who rated the manager disagreed about a specific performance dimension, this inconsistency was pointed out in the manager's readiness plan. In these cases, the plan noted that the manager should consider reasons for the differences in opinions, and whether the manager treated some subordinates differently, perhaps giving some more support than others for good reasons or not (i.e., showing favoritism).

Several workshops were designed to focus on business problems drawing on the leadership assessments and what leaders would need to do to improve employee engagement and make the company more innovative and successful. Employee survey results were used to start each session. At the outset of the program, a C-level executive thanked everyone for stepping up and doing the hard work necessary to change the trajectory and improve employee engagement. The workshops included case examples from real work problems the organization faced. Observers (other trainers) rated participants as they engaged in discussions about the problems and role-play simulations. Later, participants rated each other. The observers gave participants feedback on the ratings. The ultimate tests were future survey results and improvement in business results.

Coupling leadership skills with business problems and the economic pressures on the company made this a generative learning process, and for some managers, transformative. Business as usual was not acceptable. If the company was going to grow rather than decline, leaders needed to generate new ways of operating—efficiencies, improved customer service, and innovations in products. New marketing strategies were needed to open new markets and convey the value of the company's products relative to the competition. The consultant designed workshop sessions about leaders' roles in engaging and developing employees, being open to new ideas, and involving employees and customers in innovation, thinking through standard operations, barriers and problems in operational efficiency, best practices in the industry with an eye toward the competition, and their willingness to listen to and try new ideas.

CONCLUSION

To summarize, learning consultants can support adaptive, generative, and transformative learning. To support adaptive learning, consultants create a climate for calculated risk and capture the learning by documenting changes in skills and knowledge. To support generative learning, they locate resources and best practices, encourage new ideas and trial-and-error learning. They act as a role models, teaching continuous quality improvement techniques, encouraging trainees to shift roles for fresh perspectives. The consultants create a climate where failure is a learning experience. They give learners time to practice, give them feedback, and help them develop routines to sustain what they learned in new practices. To support transformative learning, consultants provide mechanisms for transformation, such as dialogue and reflection. Valuable transformative learning experiences include experimenting, practicing, evaluating results, and making further changes in behaviors in a continuous process of improvement and innovation. Cases 4.1 to 4.3 were examples of adaptive, generative, and transformative learning. Case 4.4 was an example of a problem-based learning intervention to increase innovation in the organization. Case 4.5 showed how the consultant used psychologically based individual assessments to identify learning needs and readiness to learn. This led the consultant to design a series of learning interventions to support leadership development. Next, in Chapter 5, we turn to how consultants apply learning theory in designing interventions that draw on the ever-increasing and often bewildering range of learning methods and technologies.

5

Learning Architecture: Integrating Technology Into Effective Interventions

Learning architecture is the set of methods for needs analysis, learning delivery, and assessments of learning outcomes in an organization. Here we focus on learning technologies. Learning professionals need to find the right delivery options to match the intended content, audience, and environment. This might be classroom training, online learning through computer or mobile technologies, on-the-job learning, or combinations thereof. In-person instructors can vary the speed of presentations to match participants' questions and other indicators of their grasp of the information. Online adaptive software can vary speed without slowing down fast learners. Online communications media can aid recall and retention and promote concept formation as well as higher order thinking (Fahy, 2008; Mayer, 2001). Graphics can be used to emphasize critical details. Video-conferencing can add a sense of direct involvement. Synchronous interactive events can increase learner engagement.

http://dx.doi.org/10.1037/0000094-006
Learning Interventions for Consultants: Building the Talent That Drives Business, by M. London and T. Diamante

The consultant can draw from existing materials, many of which are high quality and readily available for no or low cost, such as TED talks (https://www.ted.com/). Universities produce short videos about a wide range of topics and make them available on the web for little or no cost. Stanford University's website (https://www.gsb.stanford.edu/insights/ten-popular-business-videos-2015) includes videos of faculty, alumni, and guest speakers sharing insights on leadership and innovation among other topics. MIT's "Learning Edge" (https://mitsloan.mit.edu/LearningEdge/Pages/default.aspx) is a free resource for management educators with videos on topics such as entrepreneurship, leadership, ethics, operations management, strategy, corporate social responsibility, environmentally sustainable business, and system dynamics. Learning consultants need to establish criteria for adapting material from such sources. Criteria might include the clarity of the presentations, their length, their inclusion of demonstrations (not just talking points), and their relation to other methods that may be part of the training program.

CASE 5.1: USING TECHNOLOGIES FOR GLOBAL TRAINING

A global financial institution was experiencing difficulties in adhering to U.S. labor laws in different countries while complying with local laws outside the United States. The institution had offices in 25 locations in five countries. With global responsibility came the problem of standardization and enforcement. In the United States, this included policy interpretation and understanding of the federal equal employment opportunity laws, affirmative action, the Americans With Disabilities Act, the Family and Medical Leave Act, and related employee relations challenges. Despite best efforts, management had difficulty getting all offices on the same page in recognizing that they needed to comply with U.S. laws regardless of whether the office was in the United States or abroad.

The project relied on an intricate network of connection capability among the company's locations. A consultant with knowledge of labor laws as well as training was hired to craft learning materials. The consultant recognized the importance of including examples of the gray areas between a law as written and practices or circumstances that challenged what seemed straight-forward on paper. The training was delivered by the consultant in a series of webinars streamed live in three sessions, each lasting 1 hour, held on three successive Fridays at midday Central Standard Time, so participants in Asia would be online early in the morning and those in Europe would be online in the evening. The participants, about 50 in all, were executives in human resources (HR), risk management, internal audit, and compliance from around the globe. As the expert trainer lectured, participants posed questions in an online chat box displayed on a screen in the main online "training room." The most compelling part of the training occurred when policy explanations stopped and participants asked questions about challenging situations. With global livestreaming, expert lecture, online polling to be sure participants understood various points, chat for questions and answers, and discussions about pressing employee relations challenges, the training was engaging and intense. The sessions were fast paced, well-rehearsed, and the software was tested to be sure there were no technical glitches.

THE VALUE OF TECHNOLOGY FOR LEARNING INTERVENTIONS

The emergence of new technologies offers many benefits. Consider the following.

Learner Control and Self-Regulation

Learning technologies have the potential to increase learner control (self-regulation). Learners have access to information, demonstrations, and even personal contacts when they want or need them at a touch of a button. This can supplement instruction or be the primary mechanisms for delivering instruction. For instance, videos and websites on new methods, guidelines, procedures, policies, or regulations can be ready when the learner needs the information. Learners can find the information on their own, or guides can direct the learners to the information and "how-to" instructions. A challenge with the vast array of learning opportunities and methods is knowing when to use them—and what is good, and what is not. This is the job of the learning consultant. The learning consultant can develop these guides to facilitate learning and supplement traditional classroom or on-the-job training. People who are self-regulated, mastery learners will need less guidance than those who are not naturally inquisitive and open to learning all they can to perform as well as possible. Others will need to be spoon-fed through structured, step-by-step instructions. E-learning systems can offer access to people who can be available for a telephone call or online conversation at specific times if not around the clock.

Consultants recognize that learning systems will be used differently by different people, and the consultant should capitalize on design system components that are flexible or resonate with learner needs. The learning consultant can assess learners' needs and capabilities and design flexible methods that address different learning styles and goals. A website for a learning program can be developed to provide information in different ways. For instance, the site may include an introductory video, user descriptions of successful applications and problems, how-to guides with examples, simulations with realistic problem scenarios, and resources for further information. Segments can be organized on their own web pages like chapters in a textbook, with deeper information as the learner progresses. Tests or "check-in" points can occur along the way to ensure that learners are grasping the new knowledge, and learners who need more practice can be redirected to earlier information that is repeated, perhaps in a different way so as to maintain the learner's attention and/or present the same information in a novel way to enhance memory and comprehension.

Motivation

Technology allows the incorporation of motivational methods, such as goal setting, into the learning. For instance, participants can be asked to set goals for how quickly they will complete learning modules, how many they will complete, what scores they will attain on tests, and how much they will increase the intended outcomes (those that can be measured objectively, such as sales). Learning consultants provide goal setting and feedback to increase participants' engagement and learning (Locke & Latham, 2013). Measures of individual differences might be included, such as mastery learning (an orientation to be open to new ideas and continuous learning; Dweck, 1986), core self-efficacy (the feeling of being able to bring about positive outcomes; Judge, Erez, Bono, & Thoresen, 2003), and personality factors (e.g., the Big Five: Conscientiousness, Openness to experience, Agreeableness, Extraversion, and Emotional stability; McAdams & Pals, 2006; McCrae & John, 1992). These measures could be indicators of motivation to learn. For instance, participants who are low in these personality measures may need more engaging or inviting learning methods, such as face-to-face training and coaching, whereas participants who are high on the measures will likely be more receptive to self-paced learning.

Technology allows the consultant to design the pace and content of learning to optimize learner interest. The use of multiple media to deliver training addresses the short attention span of some learners, engaging them in different ways. The training can include components for learners who thrive on explanation and those who thrive on hands-on experiences and chances for experimentation (following Kolb's learning model; Kolb, 1976, 1981, 2015; Kolb, Osland, & Rubin, 1995a, 1995b; see Chapter 4). Learners who are intrinsically motivated to learn may need little more than access to training in new skills and knowledge to participate fully. As such, learners can have the opportunity to select different ways to proceed through learning content. The learning professional's responsibility is to understand how different media are used by learners and understand how learners' preferences for and interests in different training modalities are working to convey the content and achieve desired learning outcomes.

Learners who are extrinsically motivated may enjoy games that offer opportunities for rewards, recognition, or competition. As mentioned above, learning professionals can build in adaptive learning protocols so that learners can proceed through modules at their own pace. The programs can be designed so that learners select their own modes of learning, for instance, opting to participate in an online game or to answer a set of multiple choice questions and compete with other learners for the highest score.

As learners progress, they learn not only the material but also their preferences for different ways of learning. They might discover that they enjoy a game in which they compete with other learners for rewards as they acquire knowledge, for instance, answering questions that ask them to apply their learning to different problems. Other learners may find competition stressful and prefer to progress through the material on their own. Learners who have had exposure to the material previously might prefer to review written material quickly as a refresher and find spending time on simulated problem solving unnecessary. The consultant's initial needs analysis is likely to identify which learning methods are likely to be most valuable given the learners' prior knowledge and assessment of their preferred learning styles. However, when there are many learners with different levels of experiences and backgrounds, consultants can offer a range of learning options with adaptive functions that allow learners to progress in ways that match their abilities and/or preferred ways to learn (Pashler, McDaniel, Rohrer, & Bjork, 2009).

Use of Multiple Media

Technologies allow combining multiple media, including webinars, videos, simulations and games on computers and apps, and cloud-based learning software. This can make the learning more engaging than would be the case from a stand-up lecture or a video of a "talking head." Learners can weave through online program components. They do not necessarily have to follow the components in a rigid, linear way but can explore on their own as they gain a better understanding of the new skills or processes and try them on the job. This may lead to some early failures that could have been avoided by following a more structured path through the learning system, but the mistakes or errors can be vivid learning experiences. This, of course, will not work when the cost of mistakes is high, in which case, methods that require demonstration of foundation knowledge and skills will be necessary before the learning is allowed to continue—all the more reason for a learning consultant to design the learning in relation to importance to the organization and the learners.

Data Collection from Different Sources

Technology allows learning consultants to incorporate data collection mechanisms into learning programs. HR systems can record employee demographic characteristics (e.g., age) and experiences, as well as their skills, knowledge, and participation in formal learning experiences within and outside the organization (e.g., courses taken, degrees received, certificates obtained, workshops attended). These data can be used for learning needs analyses as well as for employee placement and an assessment of current and anticipated talent gaps, for instance, as a result of an aging workforce. The learning consultant can collect data on learning progress to assess the quality of learning programs across participants and use the information to improve learning outcomes. When electronic means are used to deliver education (e.g., through a webinar or website), the consultant can collect data about the use of each element of the system (e.g., the number of times the same participant viewed a demonstration video and which parts of the video the participant repeated). Participants' activities in games and simulations have records, informing the consultant about elements of the learning media that are more or less effective across participants. Software can inform the learning consultant about how much time participants spent and their performance on different facets of a game; this information could be useful to suggest improvements. In addition, participants can record their reactions to learning experiences, providing the consultants with data on their attitudes toward the training. The learning consultant can use this information to determine the extent to which the learning methods are being used, whether participants understand the material, how well participants are proceeding as they go through the material, whether they apply their learning, and whether they retain the learning over time. The learning consultant can refine and improve the learning intervention and demonstrate to the client whether the learning has met the client's expectations. Moreover, data can inform instructional design by demographic breakdowns, geographic preferences, cultural preferences, and/or other segments that might implicate a need or way to improve how learning is delivered.

Consultants can also relate participation in training to outcomes on the job, such as promotions, performance ratings, and turnover, answering such questions as: Does the training improve an employees' readiness for advancement and future success in a more responsible position 6 months or a year after training? Are employees more likely to participate in learning programs if other employees have participated? Does the training help to improve departmental outcomes? Does the training help departments respond to unexpected events in the future compared to departments that did not receive training? Do simulations speed business execution?

These questions indicate that data alone (e.g., records of participation) are likely to be of little value unless they are part of action research that compares participation and results to standards or to comparison groups, especially if the trainees and comparison group employees are followed over time. Technology allows for meaningful assessment, and learning consultants have the background to design meaningful research programs to fine tune and evaluate the success of their interventions. That being said, the learning consultant needs to understand the organizational context and the competitive situation of the business unit(s) affected by the training if not the entire enterprise. Context is critical. Purpose matters more than technology. The learning consultant must take care not to be too enthusiastic about technology and overlook the need to realize outcomes.

File Sharing for Collaboration

Technology allows file sharing for participant collaboration. Using cloud-based drives, participants in remote locations can access software to collaborate on slide presentations, documents, spreadsheet analyses, graphic image programs, and the like. This can be valuable in team learning as participants work together on one or more learning challenges. It can also be useful for learning architecture for collaboration with other learning consultants, managers, and prospective participants in getting reactions to and revising learning materials. In addition, uploading components of learning for a given learning program or multiple programs for different purposes can be a way to display an organization's learning architecture.

Communication Channels for Networking and Building Community

Technologies can establish communication channels for networking and building community within and between teams and organizations. The consultant can facilitate team development by using software that allows participants to create and expand their own learning communities (e.g., shared drives on the cloud or an online group). This is beneficial in that team leaders and members pay attention to learning they need to perform more efficiently and effectively. Moreover, teams can learn from other teams. Team members can share experiences with other members and other teams, and different teams can share approaches to problems. This is especially valuable in multiteam systems, such as military operations and emergency response teams (e.g., police units, firefighters, emergency medical technicians, government offices). Leaders of multiteam systems can learn to promote information sharing and collaboration, including posting and sharing training documents and data from simulations and actual experiences (e.g., battles or emergencies; Asencio & DeChurch, 2017; DeChurch & Marks, 2006).

Individuals can collaborate with others to tackle challenges as part of the learning process. Consider how this would work. The consultant can select a problem-solving game that gives participants experience in complex problems requiring collaboration (for examples, see Cotton, 2016, as well as Paterson, 2009). The team members may be in remote locations. They are assigned the problem during a webinar, and then work on their own through communications technologies that suit them best—e-mail, on-camera or text-based group chats, social media, teleconferences via voice-over Internet, cloud-based file sharing, web pages, and so on.

Essentially, they establish their own communication network. This network may continue after the training, as members benefit from and strengthen their learning community by interacting with team members one-to-one and/or in events for the entire team, such as monthly online meetings to share experiences and discuss challenges. The consultant can be part of this network, monitor interactions, provide explanations and resources as questions or the need for additional learning arise. As such, the consultant's involvement in the team learning intervention can be an ongoing process, at least as long as the team perceives the consultant to add value and the client is willing to maintain the consultancy. Indeed, highly effective process consultations are marked by teams eventually owning better ways of interacting as if the third-party facilitator were no longer relevant. This is transfer of ownership for sharing, reflecting, and teaching. The learning consultant can build team dynamics that support these exchanges to ensure a sustainable learning environment, real or virtual.

Access Anytime, Anywhere, on Any Device

Technology gives learners access to learning interventions anytime, anywhere through multiple devices—computers, tablets, minitablets and smartphones, so learning materials and programs can be readily available without expensive facilities and travel. Learners can participate in asynchronous learning programs on their own time. In addition, synchronous online classrooms with participants interacting with an instructor and among themselves can increase engagement. The consultant builds on these technologies for taking advantage of learners' motivation to learn (self-regulation) and for tracking participation and success.

Low-Risk, Realistic Environments
for Experimentation and Practice

Technology provides low-risk opportunities to try new skills and demonstrate new knowledge. Progress tests demonstrate learning. Participants can receive feedback on their responses, with wrong choices generating more information in an adaptive learning process. Simulations and games add realism and excitement to learning. Team problem solving, especially the challenge of a real organizational problem, can be a learning experience. However, when executives pose the problems as a learning experience and judge individual or team solutions, risks for the trainees emerge. Learning becomes intertwined with the impressions executives and team members form and can trouble the participants, impeding the knowledge/skill acquisition. Learning consultants can include dynamics such as this into the experience itself, essentially enabling participants to learn how they learn in an organizational context (i.e., under pressure, when risk is perceived to be high, when judgment of others is feared, and/or when training outcomes—real or imagined—are viewed as influencing career progression).

Learners can progress from no-risk simulations, in which responses are anonymous and used solely for learning, to team-based simulations that are opportunities to apply new knowledge to real work challenges even if still part of the learning program. The consultant, as learning architect, can balance risk to participants throughout the process and be sure that participants are aware of the implications of their behavior in the learning experience for placement, promotion, or other decisions that might be made about them.

CASE 5.2: E-PLATFORM SKILL BUILDING FOR CONFLICT AND STRESS REDUCTION

Conflict was high at one utility company. Line management was experiencing an unusually heightened level of anger, frustration, and resentment from field operations. The root cause of this hostility was multifaceted, including restructured regions and reduced staffing, especially in management ranks, while the amount of work to be done did not change. In the utility business, mistakes are not a good thing. The level of conflict grew to a point where verbal assaults turned into schoolyard bullying and violent threats. A learning intervention was needed.

Realizing that underlying causes of managers' and employees' frustration and consequent anger lay in organizational change, the vice president for human resources retained a consultant to design a workshop to address the issues. The learning was aimed at both explaining the current status of the change initiatives and the value of being more civil to each other. There was no place in the reconfigured organization for unhealthy conflict. Management and union officials came together to produce a video to kick off a self-paced information delivery and training program in a series of online modules. The first module focused on the organizational changes and stresses on the job. The next module addressed handling conflict and the human response to stress triggered by role overload, role ambiguity, and uncertain job security. The training content reinforced the policy of no tolerance for aggressive acts or utterances, and included self-management strategies to handle stresses and strains of work life. A third online module focused on courtesy, civility, and team rapport. It included a series of self-paced exercises based on examples HR managers gave to the consultant.

Several indicators were tracked to evaluate the effectiveness of the program. First, a survey of participants measured the perceived value of the content and quality of delivery. Second, employee calls to the employee assistance department were tracked to see if there was a reduction in incidents of employees feeling stressed. Finally, cases of employees reporting verbal abuse and instances of violence were tracked.

Survey results were moderately positive. Within the first 3 months after the training, calls to the employee assistance provider increased by 10%, leveled out by Month 6, and then dropped by 30% by the end of the year. This was accounted for by heightened awareness of the organizational changes leading to better self-management. The reduction in the number of reported incidents (there is no indication that workers simply failed to report) was taken as a genuine sign that the skills training was worth every nickel. The company offered refresher self-efficacy training and anonymous mechanisms to encourage employees to report conflicts. Also, the company held town hall meetings to inform employees about subsequent organizational changes and give employees a chance to convey their concerns.

TECHNOLOGY-BASED LEARNING APPLICATIONS

A variety of software systems and methods are available to support learning. Here, we consider a number of them and describe how they can be used to advance and assess learning.

Talent Management Systems

A talent management system records employees' participation in training classes and workshops offered by the organization or outside the organization. It can also record competencies associated with the learning. It will likely include employees' degrees and other academic credit. A talent management system may be part of a larger, enterprise-wide HR management system that has modules on employee characteristics (e.g., age, degrees, current and prior jobs held), or it could be separate software used by the organization. The system may be managed by the HR or training department. Managers throughout the organization—and employees—may have access to the system. Data may be posted by employees themselves, who are then accountable for the data's accuracy. The system may handle registration for internal workshops and record attendance and course completions. Employees can submit information about participation in learning outside the organization, submitting documentation to their manager or the HR or training department to certify participation. Such a system needs to be maintained. Managers can search the database to identify people who have the skills and knowledge needed for a particular assignment. Learning professionals can help design talent management systems and use them to assess learning needs as job requirements change and consultants are hired to address learning.

Across employees and departments, data on skills and knowledge in the organization can be used to examine developmental needs relative to organizational goals. The consultant might be asked to assess the organization's readiness to move in a new strategic direction, such as to implement a new customer relationship management system. Analysis of the learning database can indicate whether employees in different departments have the acumen to perform, and whether training is needed.

Other rapid analytics can include demographic information, such as experience levels and ages of employees. An analysis of the ages of employees in different job categories would indicate percentages of people who are retirement eligible. Learning consultants may conduct such analyses as part of a learning needs assessment. These data would be useful for determining future hiring needs and whether the organization should develop training programs for current employees or embark on recruiting new employees who already have the needed skills and knowledge, which in turn might suggest the need for improved orientation training for new employees.

A talent management system is also valuable for employees to track their own accomplishments. This is especially useful if the organization is posting job opportunities that include educational requirements and specific skill and knowledge expectations. Employees can readily see the extent to which they meet the requirements for specific job openings. Also, the system can generate data about education and skills. The consultant can write summaries of educational and training needs and expectations in the organization or business unit. The consultant can build career paths, rotational job assignments, ad hoc action teams, coaching programs, and other in-house means to nurture and develop talent.

The consultant can also track the use of the system itself to determine its value to the organization. Are employees using it? Do employees need training on the system itself? Would reminders to employees that the system is available be useful? Reminders could give employees examples of how they can use the system in conjunction with postings of job openings, online seminars, management education workshops, external educational opportunities as well as information about organizational goals and how intellectual capital leads to competitive advantage. (For examples of the design and implementation of talent management systems in different organizations see Cannon's 2016 case study of the U.S. Navy's talent management system; Moon and Lee's 2017 description of a new talent management system for public officials; Naim and Lenka's 2017 application of a talent management system in the IT industry; and Meyers and von Woerkom's 2014 overview of talent management systems applications.)

Learning Management Systems

Learning management systems (LMSs) are for trainers and learning consultants to develop and deliver customized, electronically based training (e-learning). They include authoring software for designing a wide variety of learning resources, including videos, games, simulations, informational resources, and tests. The coding capability of the LMS enables access to computers, smartphones, and tablets, making learning more convenient and portable. LMSs include platforms for online learning with components for registration, announcements, assignments, discussion boards, links to resources, communication with individual students or groups of students, online student meetings, subgrouping students for team learning and collaboration, testing, grading, and surveying to assess learners' opinions about the program or issues addressed by the program. (See Toth, 2015, for an overview of learning management systems for online learning.)

Employee Networks and Interest Groups

Technology can maintain networks that support employees controlling their own learning. A network might operate within a social media interest group, forum, or blog on topics such as emerging technologies, competitive forces in an industry, or how to use a particular software program. Forums can be internal to the organization, affiliated with a professional association, or just an ad hoc group initiated by an individual (perhaps the consultant) based on shared interests or concerns on matters of learning technology. These learning communities can be used to communicate advances in technology. Members can pose and answer each other's "how-to" questions. The risk, of course, is that information people convey to each other may not be accurate. Within an organization, however, forums can be monitored and inaccuracies corrected.

Learning consultants can encourage learner networks and interest groups by providing methods for communication, such as blogs, so that all students (and others outside a learning program) can follow participants' comments about what they are learning. Learning professionals can analyze internal blogs or forums to capture the pulse and climate of the organization. The analysis might yield information on workforce training needs. For instance, as part of implementing a training course, whether online or in person, the consultant can incorporate an e-network so that participants can share experiences about the topic of the workshop with discussions about how well they are implementing what they are learning and how the training program might be improved.

Networks pose the risk of learners cheating on competency criterion measures or sharing information about items and their answers. If testing is involved, students can be warned and asked to adhere to integrity policies. Different learners may receive different forms of tests. Learning professionals can monitor communications. Software in learning management systems can determine the percentage of overlap, if any, of a learner's work with that of other sources, including published works and written work of the other learners in the class or in other classes. (Turnitin.com and Safeassign.com are examples of such software, available as part of a learning system, such as Blackboard.com, or as standalone software.)

Simulations and Virtual Worlds

Virtual worlds are computer-based simulated environments. Participants "attend" as avatars, interacting with others in the simulation. The virtual world can also be a virtual classroom, with the student as avatar participating by asking questions of the instructor, holding small group discussions with other participants in chat rooms, and demonstrating learned skills in the simulated environment. Virtual worlds are useful for reproducing semirealistic complex environments, such as hospital operating rooms, buildings, engines, and even battles in remote territories. (Secondlife.com is an example of a virtual world.) Participants, acting as themselves or playing roles, interact as they learn. They meet other participants and try newly learned behaviors. Although there is no end to the creation of these simulated environments and their value for training, they require expert instructional technologists, software designers, and coders, and (not surprisingly) are expensive to design and produce. Learning consultants can work with designers to highlight the central elements to be learned, determine the extent of realism necessary (cartoon-like drawings may be fine for many applications), and include demonstrations, interactions with the instructor and other participants, practice opportunities, and testing.

Artificial Intelligence and Automation

Artificial intelligence (AI) uses data analytics and simulations to help solve real work problems (Borana, 2016; Greenwald, 2017). AI ranges from high-skill tasks, such as recognizing cancer in X-ray images, to lower skill tasks, such as recognizing text in images. Automation uses machines (robotics) to do routine and complex tasks. Learning consultants may be asked to train employees for AI and automated work. A White House report (Executive Office of the President, 2016) described how AI and automation are stimulating the imperative to educate and train Americans for jobs of the future: "As AI changes the nature of work and the skills demanded by the labor market, American workers will need to be prepared with the education and training that can help them continue to succeed. . . . Assisting U.S. workers in successfully navigating job transitions will . . . become increasingly important; this includes expanding the availability of job-driven training and opportunities for lifelong learning" (p. 3). The report pointed to technical skills such as software development and computer engineering. There will be more jobs in generating, collecting, and managing data to feed into AI training without intervention to help them reskill.

In addition to preparing people for AI and automation work applications, learning consultants can incorporate AI applications in training design. Adaptive learning is a form of AI that has the advantage of assessing students' learning and directing them to clarifying information or new material depending on their progress (Truong, 2016). Measures of learners' strengths and weaknesses at the start and along the way can channel the learners through material that fits their learning style, repeating content and assessments in different ways as needed, so that learners proceed at their own pace.

Learning professionals can create chatbots or virtual agents as job aids to supplement training. Widely used in customer service interfaces, employees can query a virtual agent through voice-controlled mobile or online technology when issues arise or when they need to know how some process or equipment works. The computer can respond with prepared answers and "learn" in the process about what issues arise frequently, what combinations of answers are most responsive, and the experience and job conditions of employees who are asking these questions. (For information about how to design and use chatbots, see Yao, 2017.)

AI allows learning professionals to measure use of learning and to track needs for learning (Greenwald, 2017). It can search candidates for job openings, identifying people in the organization or other organizations who have acquired needed skills and can be recruited for positions. AI can assess performance and attitudes by collecting data from electronic communications (with the knowledge of the observed employees), discovering issues, trends, and behavioral tendencies that suggest directions for improved operations. Learning consultants can draw on this information to design more effective training or deliver online training when employees need it.

Games

Companies are using serious games to develop talent. Kelly (2013) offered the following definitions: A *game* is "a competitive activity that involves skill, chance, or endurance" (p. 2). A *simulation* is a game that attempts to represent real situations. A *serious game* is one designed especially for learning. An *alternative reality game* uses player interactions that represent the real world, often incorporating multiple media to tell a story. An MMORPG is a *massively multiplayer online role-playing game.*

Gamification is the incorporation of game characteristics into learning as a way to motivate and engage learners (Zichermann & Cunningham, 2011). Elements of games may include stories, goals, feedback, and play. Games can reinforce skills, provide instruction, give practice opportunities, performance feedback, and, overall, enhance learners' use of the training content. Gamification applications for learning appear to be expanding.

A survey of 551 business and learning leaders conducted in 2013 by i4cp and ASTD found that 25% reported that their companies are using gamification in learning, and another 25% said they are planning to pursue gamification in some way (ASTD Research, 2014; Morrison, 2016).

Virtual worlds can be extended to include games with multiple participants and layers of difficulty. Each layer can require additional skills, with the game adding excitement and motivating learners to achieve and "win," possibly for rewards. The learning consultant can break down the skills and knowledge to be learned into game components, incorporate problems to be solved and barriers to overcome, and establish reinforcement contingencies (systems for points to be earned and prizes to be won).

Online games can also work well for team-building exercises, dividing a large group into teams or having teams from different departments compete. After the game, or at various points along the way, the learning consultant as facilitator can discuss with participants topics such as leadership, cooperation within and between teams, the motivational value of competition, negotiation processes, and conflict resolution strategies to name a few possibilities. Also, games can be used to understand empathy and problem solving from multiple perspectives. Participants can switch roles at various points, letting them see the game from others' perspectives. And participants can give each other feedback to help them learn about their risk taking, aggressiveness, decision-making, and communication skills and abilities.

Games offer learning experiences in safe, simulated environments that are especially valuable in high-risk situations such as health care and the military (Kelly, 2013). As players interact in games, they can develop skills like emotional intelligence, communication, problem solving, collaboration, and leadership. Video games and 3-D virtual reality games can increase perceptual and cognitive abilities, including information processing and memory (Kapp, 2010, 2016a, 2016b). Such technology can simulate complex tasks that require coordinated efforts. An example is the U.S. Army's *First Person Cultural Trainer*. It uses a 3-D simulation that places players in unfamiliar communities and requires them to learn social structures and work with community members to accomplish missions. (This simulation was developed with the University of Texas at Dallas School of

Arts, Technology, and Emerging Communication. For information about the simulation, contact the Center [http://www.utdallas.edu/atec/]; see also Kelly, 2013; Roth, 2011.) The game replicates physical expressions, teaches the effects of speech, body language, posture, temperament, and action, and gives learners experiences for resolving conflicts.

While serious games provide a nonthreatening, realistic environment for action learning, "casual" games (readily available online games that have simple rules and little demands on time or skills) are increasingly popular in corporate learning. Kapp (2016a) reported on a 12-month study of casual games played by 6,301 retail associates using a software platform that tracked learner performance on the game. In one retail organization, at the start of each short (30 seconds) delivery of training materials, employees could choose to play a minigame lasting up to 2 minutes. The game resumed after each segment of learning. Learners who correctly answered the quiz questions about the topic in the game segment were awarded up to 10 seconds of bonus game time per correct question. In the other organization, employees did not have the option of playing a game before being exposed to the learning content and the quiz for each segment. The learners in the game condition logged in to train more often, answered more questions correctly, and had longer correct answer streaks than learners in the no-game condition. "Playing the casual game seemed to place the learner in a state of flow—a mental state in which a person is fully immersed and focused in what they are doing—and allowed them to concentrate more fully on a question after they had played the game for a few moments" (Kapp, 2016a, p. 51). The game increased alertness, vigilance, memory, and openness to learning. Learning professionals could conduct research into whether these benefits transferred to the job and lasted.

CASE 5.3: EXAMPLE OF GAMIFICATION AND CORPORATE CHANGE

Gale (2016) reported on the use of a game by BBVA Bancomer, the largest financial institution in Mexico, when it moved the 9,500 employees from its headquarters with traditional private offices to a state-of-the-art building with open work spaces designed to increase collaboration and environmental systems to save energy and recycle. The company used gamification, social media, and live actors to transform their traditional organization culture into "a collaborative, environmentally focused digital organization" (Gale, 2016, p. 44). Employees were moved in stages of about 100 people at a time on the same floor so that the training created camaraderie and offered mutual support.

Online gamification was used to foster collaboration and competition. It included online training, social media elements, and real activities comprising 14 "missions" in three phases over 12 weeks. The first phase was aimed at building awareness of the need for new behaviors. Employees watched a video about respecting the environment and participated in an online trivia game about problem solving and collaboration. The second phase was about taking action on the job. Employees performed specific assignments, such as scheduling a shared meeting space. The third phase was about reflection and feedback. During this phase, discussions occurred on an internal social media platform, and participants completed feedback surveys and described examples of team members working more collaboratively. Throughout, employees earned points for task completion. They could exchange points for prizes and also receive badges as they earned higher rankings that showed levels of mastery.

Comparison of survey results before and after the move showed improvements in attitudes about embracing technology and paying attention to work–life balance. The company recognized that follow up was needed to reinforce the environment where employees could learn from each other as they fostered collaboration and innovation. This is an example of the fusion of technology, learning, and behavior change as a tactic to create a culture that can sustain a more competitive environment. Such learning methods will likely become an avenue of increased study and practice by consultants.

CASE 5.4: BLENDING MODES OF DELIVERY

A consulting psychologist was hired to design, implement, and evaluate a program to train supervisors to be better coaches and developers of their subordinates. The consultant had previously been hired to work with the HR staff to revise the firm's performance appraisal process for supervisors. They revised the annual performance appraisal to include how well supervisors perform the role of coach and developer with evidence from subordinate ratings (e.g., subordinate responses to items such as "My supervisor spends time telling me about career opportunities in the company," and "My supervisor gives me a chance to learn new skills that will improve my chances for advancement"). The appraisals included judgments of higher level managers who observe supervisors' interactions with their team members. The appraisals also collected data on use of educational resources (e.g., sending subordinates to training, giving subordinates a chance to try new tasks and assignments). However, the role of coach and developer had not been incorporated into the performance measurement process previously, and the consulting psychologist recommended to the company's vice president for human resources that supervisors needed training and coaching on this new expectation.

E-mails to supervisors directed them to sites on the firm's intranet website about the role of supervisor as coach and developer and explained that supervisors would be evaluated annually on how well they performed this role. The site included (a) a description of the role and how it is included in the performance appraisal (ratings from subordinates and the supervisor's manager); (b) examples of outstanding performance, good performance, and poor performance in the role; (c) videos of supervisors having a coaching session with a subordinate modeling each performance level; and (d) dates for a 2-hour workshop that supervisors were expected to attend.

Workshops were led by the consulting psychologist with a senior manager as a coleader. They emphasized the importance that the organization placed on employee development. Each workshop included demonstrations, time for discussion (including asking participants about mentoring they have had themselves during their careers), reviews of competencies that are important to the organization (e.g., knowledge of variables affecting the company's financial success, customer relationships, and learning resources and tuition assistance that the company offers employees), and time to role-play one-to-one coaching sessions. A webinar version of the workshop was offered for supervisors in the company's regional offices. This avoided travel expenses while giving all supervisors a chance to receive the training. The webinar included chat rooms for questions and answers. The webinar used the same slide presentations and general format as the in-person workshop, except that the webinar participants needed to observe a demonstration role-play rather than participate in one. In addition to this training, local executives were trained to lead discussions with the supervisors who reported to them about giving feedback and coaching for performance improvement and career development of their subordinate team members.

After the supervisors participated in the training and used the new performance appraisal form, the company updated the intranet website every quarter to include average subordinates' and managers' ratings of supervisors' performances in the role of supervisor as coach and developer. The website included a discussion board for supervisors to post opinions and observations about what coaching styles worked best and how supervisors could plan for employee training without reducing team performance because of employee time away from the job during training.

The takeaway for learning consultants is that blending modes of delivery can provide training and behavior measurement to reinforce a culture change, in this case, one that was integral to the organization's performance management policies. The initial survey results pointed to the need for training. The website provided information and guidelines. Workshops were an opportunity for experiential learning. The webinar brought cost-effective training to distant locations. The online dashboard evaluated the success of the program and provided feedback to managers. The dashboard enabled measurement of results so that follow-up workshops could reinforce the role of manager as coach and developer of talent. The success of the multipronged, technology-based learning rather than a single workshop experience suggests that learning consultants can take a comprehensive approach to learning that occurs over time and that reaches individuals in different ways.

CONCLUSION

Technology is changing the way learning occurs. The wide range of technologies available and the many ways they can be configured provides an amazing array of learning options. Together, learning technologies can foster clarity of purpose, efficiency of delivery, learning style preferences, and employee accountability for participating and applying learning.

Learning technologies offer options for increased learner engagement in all aspects of the learning process, combining traditional in-person learning, access to information and demonstrations, opportunities to test learners' knowledge, and means for continuous learning. In Chapter 6, we address the implications this changing world of learning has for new learning applications, research, and expanded challenges for learning consultants.

6

Recommendations, Challenges, and Directions for the Future

Learning consultants can diagnose learning needs, readiness, and potential. They can do this from the standpoint of individuals, teams, and organizations. They have the expertise to measure individuals' abilities and motivations, as well as team and organizational conditions that may require acquisition of new skills and knowledge, especially during times of change. Learning professionals also keep an eye on competitive challenges and organizational demands outside of the organization that indicate the need for learning inside the organization. Given the many ways that consultants as learning professionals contribute to employee development, we conclude the book with a set of recommendation, challenges, and directions for the future.

The approaches the learning consultant uses depend on such factors as the organization's and participants' readiness for change, openness to new ideas, likelihood of accepting feedback and coaching, and

http://dx.doi.org/10.1037/0000094-007
Learning Interventions for Consultants: Building the Talent That Drives Business, by M. London and T. Diamante

resources for rewards to reinforce new behaviors. In addition, the state of the business, its competitive situation and its sense of urgency accelerate or impede the consultant's efforts to drive a learning initiative. So the consultant has to have a good understanding of the organization to begin with—hence the importance of a needs analysis that incorporates analyzing individual capabilities *and* organizational conditions and culture (Step 1: Needs Analysis). Most organizations do not exist in order to create learning experiences; therefore, the learning consultant needs to identify, articulate, and disseminate the value proposition for the educational engagement. This proposition should state how learning at the individual, team, and/or organizational level will enhance the competitive stance of the organization. In working with an organization over time, the consultant may discover that some methods of learning work better than others—hence the value of tracking participants' reactions, behavior changes, and perceptions of organization leaders once learning experiences begin. Learning consultants are advised to be ready to adjust methods to improve outcomes and to root these outcomes in core aspects of the organization, demonstrating the learning connection to critical operating objectives if not the mission of the firm (Step 5: Evaluation).

RECOMMENDATION 1: ANTICIPATE THE NEED FOR TALENT

Consultants enable leaders to be forward thinking by conducting training needs analyses and feeding back results to the organization in order to suggest avenues for learning. Assessments might draw on employees' performance appraisal results, team leaders' 360-degree performance ratings from coworkers, or managers' scores in assessment centers that evaluate their potential for advancement in the organization. Another source of information might be employees' self-assessments of capabilities, personality, values, and other relevant characteristics. Consultants then use these data to design, deliver, and evaluate various forms of training. The training may be traditional classroom, online sessions, or self-paced software. Consultants may also be coaches. They can offer support for managers' career planning, coach managers who are identified as having potential for advancement, or help executives who are derailing to get back on track. These efforts strive to improve the alignment between organizational goals and individuals' capabilities and motivation.

Consultants also can conduct analyses of future jobs. They can examine forecasts of technological, global, and economic changes with a view to the near- and long-term future, say 5 or more years ahead. Consultants can interview executives and subject matter experts about their views of trends in their industry. Also, consultants can help learners discover this information themselves and use the results for planning their continuous learning in order to remain competitive and successful in their current positions and to set career development goals. Strategic direction of the client organization requires the right people, knowing the right things, doing the right things, and learning—all the time. Some of this can be trained (e.g., skills) and some can be nurtured (e.g., curiosity, openness to new experiences), but collectively the learning consultant is building the adaptive capacity of the organization so it can grow.

Organizations may hire consultants to conduct job analyses to define requirements of future (anticipated) jobs (Frey & Osborne, 2017). Consultants can analyze job trends within and across professions and industries. They can interview industry experts—executives and professionals who are knowledgeable about trends and emerging business models, with a finger on the pulse of the competition if not directly experimenting with technological advances. They can reflect on what the organization might do and what this means for the talent the organization needs to be successful for the future. This requires data on employees' current skills, knowledge, and educational levels in different parts of the organization. Information about age and tenure in the organization indicates retirement eligibility several years ahead, suggesting future learning challenges. Consultants can use surveys, interviews, and observations to examine employees' commitment to the organization and engagement in their work. Talent is a by-product of many dimensions of work, including the challenge of the work itself, the resources available to meet those challenges (inadequate resources can lead to burnout; Bakker, Demerouti, &

Sanz-Vergel, 2014), and employees' hardiness (resistance to stress, optimism, and readiness to bounce back from failure).

RECOMMENDATION 2: SUPPORT THE DEVELOPMENT OF EMPLOYEES' CAREER MOTIVATION

An individual's career motivation can be viewed as a function of at least three factors—*resilience* (having self-confidence and the belief that they can be successful [e.g., in learning difficult skills and performing under challenging circumstances]), *insight* (being objective about personal strengths and weaknesses and knowledgeable about the strengths and weaknesses the organization wants for today and the future), and *identity* (having clear and realistic career goals and seeing oneself in advanced roles [e.g., a position of significant leadership in the organization]; Mone & London, 2010). Career insight is based on information about oneself and opportunities as they arise or are imagined. Career paths are affected by the same information, suggesting the viability of avenues worth taking to achieve goals. Along with goal setting comes commitment to these goals, and then assuming the personal sacrifice and effort or tenacity to acquire the job experiences (i.e., learning) necessary for success.

Learning professionals enable individuals to gain accurate career insight and form a meaningful (challenging and realistic) professional identity and career trajectory. Consulting psychologists can be especially helpful in this regard. They can identify viable trajectories for learning and development and design work environments that will lead to higher levels of engagement and prosperity for the individual and the organization. Consulting psychologists can uncover and help individuals overcome personal, interpersonal, and organizational obstacles to success. They do this through assessment, feedback, and counseling aimed at performance improvement and continuous learning. Employees gain an accurate view of their strengths and weaknesses from third-party, objective. and caring professionals. Under the counseling umbrella of trust and confidentiality, forthright conversations are possible, and employees can learn about career opportunities that are in line with their competencies (i.e., strengths and weaknesses), interests, emotional fortitude, and work–life goals.

RECOMMENDATION 3: IDENTIFY PAIN POINTS AND OPPORTUNITIES FOR LEARNING

Consultants can identify *learning triggers* in the organization—factors that impose pressures (or pain) indicating the need to improve performance. Consultants can help employees at all organizational levels recognize and step up to these pressures. Such pressures could be new technologies that impose a competitive threat, consequent shifts in organizational goals and/or strategies, and crises that demand the capability to act (and even think) differently. A workforce transformation initiative could be to develop mastery learners (as we discussed in Chapter 4). Employees' desire to learn and pressures or demands in the environment increase their responsiveness to training, coaching, and on-the-job learning opportunities (London & Sessa, 2007). Developing a continuous learning culture is a challenge for consultants since employees vary in their learning orientation. Some employees may thrive on learning as a competition. Others may not see themselves as able to learn, or perhaps they are not interested in expanding their job knowledge. Some may not be open to new experiences or they may defend their role or status by suggesting that the need for learning is for others in the organization but not them. The consultant can administer surveys to assess employees' learning orientation. This can inform the consultant as to whether they are speaking to an audience of, on average, mastery learners or an audience more focused on achieving immediate results. The learning audience's needs and orientation are important variables to consider as is the larger, organizational need. Gaps here—between externally driven, organizational need and employee desire—are cracks in the system and require consulting attention and eventual closure. One means to enhance a continuous learning culture is to help the organization identify employees who are mastery learners, point them out as role models, and provide readily available resources for learning. Beyond that, consulting psychologists are advised to counsel leadership to address larger systemic elements (e.g., hiring and promotion practices, performance management, culture) that may need to change.

When working with a team, the learning consultant can assess the team's readiness to learn. Teams may need to learn new operating methods and commit to new goals. Increased competition and/or emerging technologies certainly influence how teams function and how work gets done. The learning professional can be a team facilitator, working with the leader and members to guide them through discussions about change, external threats, internal operational deficiencies, and consequent goal achievement. Learning interventions for developing teams can be calibrated to enhance team cohesion, execution, and overall efficacy especially under harsh business circumstances (Silberstang & Diamante, 2008).

The learning professional can provide fine-tuned analyses of situational demands that require learning. Ignoring changes on the horizon is easy when the team is enmeshed in accomplishing routine tasks or managing daily operations. The consultant can suggest that the team take time from the daily routine—perhaps in a retreat format away from the office—to reflect on the organization and anticipate the future. Indeed, reflection—taking time to discuss observations and feelings in an environment of psychological safety and mutual trust facilitated by a consultant—is an often overlooked and grossly undervalued business asset.

Consultants address a team's readiness to learn by measuring members' open-mindedness, desire to learn, and tendency to value learning for its own sake—components of mastery learning. Consultants can also assess a team's readiness to learn by averaging measures of mastery learning across team members and examining the range (variation) across members, and/or by examining the team's past behavior in learning. Consultants can document the extent to which a team has learned and now has a higher capacity to continue to learn. The consultant can collect examples of the team's learning, what was learned and why was it necessary, perhaps documenting outcomes produced as a result of learning (as they occur), and discussing them in team meetings as a facilitated learning process. There is nothing like a tangible outcome, be it a new product or innovative solution, to make the point that learning works. The learning process used to enable outcomes deserves attention. Discussing the learning process is an opportunity for the team to pause and recognize what they have learned, give learners credit, and reflect on how the learning occurred (what worked well and what did not; Kozlowski & Salas, 2012).

RECOMMENDATION 4: BUILD ORGANIZATIONAL MECHANISMS TO SUPPORT LEARNING

The consultant can provide guidance to managers and executives about the value of learning resources and the need for ongoing support. Of course, the best way to do this is to have data to show the value of learning initiatives. Consultants can build program evaluation into contracts whenever possible. Even when data collection and analysis are not part of the contract, the learning professional would do well to provide clients with a summary report of initial results (e.g., participant performance during training; satisfaction at the conclusion of training; the resolution of problems; or the establishment of new, better directions that result from coaching sessions). Reporting these results can be an occasion for a discussion of recommendations for continued data collection to track longer term, on-the-job outcomes, in addition to assessment of future learning needs for the participants or others who did not participate in the training. In general, the learning professional can facilitate ongoing information sharing and build a culture of continuous learning that positively affects the adaptive capacity of the organization.

Organizations that foster a culture of continuous learning may rely on employees to educate each other. Learning technology provides a ready vehicle for an employee-to-employee network. For instance, at Google, 80% of training runs through a networked called "g2g" (Googler-to-Googler; see https://rework.withgoogle.com/guides/learning-development-employee-to-employee/steps/introduction/?utm_source=re:Work+Newsletter&utm_medium=email&utm_campaign=oct_newsletter). This is a volunteer network of 6,000 employees from all departments who volunteer to train their peers by teaching courses online and in person, facilitating training courses (e.g., coaching peers on training content and evaluating learning outcomes), providing one-to-one mentoring, and developing learning materials and cases. Although this might seem to make the learning consultant superfluous, training professionals are hired to deliver learning programs for top executives and to design materials and provide actionable feedback to the facilitators. A challenge for the consultant and the human resources (HR) professionals and managers in the company is to maintain the momentum for peer-to-peer learning by tracking and rewarding participation; training and giving feedback to employees who are facilitators, coaches, and mentors; evaluating outcomes; and using the results to improve learning.

RECOMMENDATION 5: IDENTIFY POSSIBLE BARRIERS TO LEARNING AND CHALLENGES FOR THE LEARNING PROFESSIONAL

There is a potential dark side to learning—things that can go wrong, barriers to learning, and unanticipated events. Also, people can learn the wrong thing. For instance, in learning ways to improve communication, they may focus on a new system for sharing files between and within teams. They may overuse file sharing, making changes to and posting the files without communicating what they did, or that they even made any changes, for instance on a project timeline. The communication tool might get overused and possibly misused, intentionally or not. Oversharing and the need to self-promote or otherwise "cover" oneself are examples that are too commonplace. Moreover, the shared file system may not work well when team members are in other countries that have cultural norms of talking through changes before they are made. Another example might be learning to conduct a constructive annual performance feedback meeting and not using the same feedback behaviors in daily interactions with subordinates. Lack of resources can be another barrier. Yet another may be employee resistance to learning, perhaps because a previous learning initiative was viewed as waste of time and money. The consultant can help to identify these barriers and suggest ways to overcome them. In addition, the consultant should look for possible barriers when they are working on a new initiative—perhaps while conducting the initial needs analysis (Step 1 of our five-step process in Chapter 3) and when discussing program options to formulate the contract (Step 2). Useful questions might be: Will supervisors be willing to send their employees to training? Will supervisors take time themselves to participate in the training? Will the organization pay to evaluate the program? Are the resources sufficient to cover the cost of development and implementation? Does the client have a realistic expectation for how long the training will take and what will be accomplished?

Consider some of the issues that a facilitator of learning may need to overcome. These include negative attitudes from participants, misguided expectations (e.g., pressure for rapid results), learning methods that do not work for everyone (e.g., some learners need more time or more opportunity to practice), poor alignment of learning with the organization (e.g., learning is not rewarded; employees are expected to meet immediate work needs and departmental goals, and are not prepared for future demands and opportunities in the organization), or learning does not match the need (e.g., because there was no opportunity to pilot test and refine the program, the situation changes, or the players who hired the consultant change over the course of a project and what seemed good at the beginning may not be later on). Some of these concerns can be anticipated and avoided by planning and embedding contingencies in a client contract. For example, a client can be convinced to include program evaluation as part of the project in the interest of knowing the return on investment, as discussed in Chapter 5. Consultants should not be timid or fearful about demonstrating the value of their efforts. Poor attitudes can be assessed before starting a project by interviewing or surveying executives, managers, or the people who are likely to participate in the learning experience about their attitudes toward the project and their desire to participate in training. HR executives, who may be the principal clients, are likely to be good sources of information about the culture and climate of the organization. The consultant might sense that the learning program should be tied to a broader organizational change effort, for instance, facilitating working relationships within and across teams or implementing a climate survey to determine employee attitudes about organizational goal clarity, leadership style, compensation and rewards, career growth, and promotional opportunities.

Inevitably, events will not unfold exactly as expected. Participants will sometimes experience unanticipated barriers to learning. Professional skills, coaching, and support will be needed. Organizational priorities can change, and consultants will then need to apply their skills to their own plans, being ready to shift the content and delivery of a learning program, possibly to delay the initiative, and/or to recommend bringing in other experts to handle challenges.

Given that situations can be uncertain and sometime chaotic, consultants need to be able to establish constructive social dynamics: safety, trust, openness to criticism, and readiness to learn. This can be important when the learning is leading employees through a course of inquiry rather than teaching defined content. The consultant can catalyze innovation by building learning environments that invite inquiry for the sake of just asking questions. There is no need to guarantee an outcome when the goal is creativity. To build learning environments that encourage a dialectic dialogue is a cultural initiative. Consultants can give learners the chance to pause, ponder, and pontificate without criticism, expectation, or a timeline.

In addition to the challenge of uncertainty, learning consultants need to recognize when emotions underlie learning content. The consultant as organizational "trainer" or even "educator" is always facing a history that reflects past learning experiences. There are individualized stories or memories relevant to the learning that is to take place, and there is an agenda or a concern that sits with every participant—usually anchored on figuring out "how best" to handle or respond to the leader or trainer in front of the room. The content of the training itself might trigger psychophysiological reactions, especially when the work is emotionally charged and may conjure up memories, fear, concerns, and possibly anger (e.g., from feelings of harassment, wrongful discrimination, litigation prevention, domestic violence, conflict, conflict management, and stress). Learning professionals are advised to measure "readiness for learning" as an openness or receptivity to new ideas and behaviors.

Yet another challenge may be changing learners' worldviews. Transforming how employees view the world is a more ambitious challenge that organizations pose to learning consultants. This need may be triggered by globalization, cross-cultural challenges, workforce demographics and morale, and more generally the disruptive nature of business and business operations. We are in an era of rethinking all kinds of business and interactive possibilities for commerce and community, and that thinking requires continuous learning mentalities and supportive environments.

RECOMMENDATION 6: BE A CONTINUOUS LEARNER

Learning consultants themselves must be continuous learners as they create learning experiences for themselves and others. They need to continue to grow and be increasingly effective and competitive. Critical thinking is the raison d'être for the profession of consulting psychology. Learning challenges will continue to expand and become more complex, and learning consultants' roles in identifying needs and designing solutions will continue to grow. To stay current with the literature on training methods, learning technologies, and organizational applications, here are some recommendations for ongoing education and self-improvement:

- Hone critical thinking skills by considering alternative strategies and evaluating outcomes of consultancies.
- Keep up with technological changes. Read about new technological applications for training. Invent and test new learning methods in relation to different individual and organizational needs.
- Ask clients and participants for feedback, not just at the conclusion of an initiative but also as the initiative progresses. For instance, ask about responsiveness, relationships with participants, how ideas and initiatives were introduced, clarity of the proposal and learning materials, value of learning outcomes and comparison to what the client expected.
- Consult with colleagues, which may require bringing a partner into a consulting project.
- Attend conferences and workshops to learn about current trends in learning, hear about innovative learning initiatives, and discuss ideas with colleagues.
- Contribute to developments in the field by participating in online forums and conferences, and publishing cases and research.
- Read about educational efforts, learning experiences, and professional development activities outside the "learning profession," as nontraditional avenues to information can often bring enlightenment.

The learning consultant of the future needs to be self-aware and up-to-date in the use and value of new technology. For instance, technology is now deployed to diagnose learning needs (e.g., collecting data from multiple sources such as employees, leaders, and users/customers) and, of course, to communicate knowledge and to enhance skill acquisition via simulations that mirror real-world circumstances. Flexibility, responsiveness, and assessment skills will be important to analyze and communicate learning needs accurately and clearly, establish realistic expectations, design learning interventions that fit the need, and evaluate outcomes.

Learning in organizations does not occur in a vacuum. There is a business or institutional need to change, and change means doing things differently. This often requires the acquisition of new knowledge and/or new skills. The context of learning is important. Learning under stress is different from learning when relaxed. Memory is also affected by state of mind. Knowing what the workforce learned and the conditions under which they learned is useful for consultants designing learning interventions. We chose this final case because it entails learning professionals' input to major organizational culture change and transformational learning.

CASE 6.1: DIVERSITY, RESPECT, CIVILITY AND THE LAW

A major software company found itself under legal scrutiny for questionable practices surrounding finances and treatment of employees. This led to a class action suit and eventually to a consent decree intended to improve practices. A new executive director was appointed by the board. The consent decree called for culture change, policy development, and training of all employees and management. These challenges were tackled by a consulting psychologist and a team of training professionals. The team realized that the workforce was skeptical, resistant, and hypervigilant. Claims of a better day coming or, more generally, anything that hinted of change was highly suspect. Messages of better days were delivered in years past but never came to be.

The learning intervention began with information gathering. The consulting psychologist and training professionals (who were skilled interviewers) interviewed a representative sample of employees across the organization. In addition, an online portal was set up for anyone to provide anonymous comments on most any matter. The data collected validated that employees were skeptical and had little hope that anything a consultant would do would really matter. The training, aimed for all management and workers, had three components: (a) policy change; (b) ethics;[1] and (c) antidiscrimination practices, interactions and practices. The team of consultants decided to create a 1-day program of cultural immersion. The themes were "welcome to the new," "shed the past," and "we know what you think about this place, so let's fix it." Signs with these phrases were posted for participants to read when they entered the room.

This was to be an intense, factual, and experiential day. It did not feel or look like training. There was a mix of education. For instance, the module on federal laws and protections was introduced as "Did you know someone cares about how you are treated at work?" New policies and revised old policies were explained and distributed in print. Examples of acceptable and unacceptable behavior anchored the policy explanations. The learning consultant introduced an ethics module that included role-plays. In this module, actors portrayed highly sensitive, illegal, and gray areas, touching upon all forms of discrimination. Vignettes were followed by discussions facilitated by a consultant. For instance, comparisons were made between how race, gender, and national origin were treated during hiring and promotion interviews.

The consultant in this case conducted an in-depth needs analysis to understand the sensitive organizational issues. Supported by other training professionals, the consultant orchestrated a change-the-culture retreat day for all employees to drive home the needed transformative culture change, incorporating different experiential learning methods. An open question immediately following the event was whether this was sufficient to stimulate the change. New behaviors need to be reinforced by management, and repeats of previously dysfunctional behaviors cannot be

---

[1]See Lowman and Cooper (2018), *The Ethical Practice of Consulting Psychology* (in this series) for more information about consulting psychologists' ethical responsibilities when working in organizational settings.

tolerated. Being accountable for designing meaningful learning interventions that addressed organizational needs, the consultant was a stimulus for learning. The learning consultant offered follow-up training and also offered to develop measures of behaviors and performance outcomes; however, the organization was not open to contracting for such work. Ultimately, the responsibility for learning and behavior change rests with the organization; if change does not occur, the consequences may threaten the organization's viability. Internal learning and HR professionals may work within the organization to support change.

Leaving the consultancy after this one major learning event was frustrating for the consultant. However, this is the nature of learning consultancies and a lesson for external consultants. The consultant and training professionals gained experience with organizational analysis and culture change that they could apply in other contexts.

CONCLUSION

We reviewed recommendations and future directions for consulting psychologists as learning professionals. These include being able to help clients (a) identify future needs for talent, (b) support and develop employees' career motivation, (c) identify pressures and opportunities for learning, (d) determine employees' perceptions of need and their readiness and capacity to learn, and (e) evaluate whether the client organization has mechanisms to support learning. We considered the dark side of learning interventions, for example, a lack of alignment of expectations, methods, and organizational conditions. As we showed in Chapter 5, emerging technologies make the future rife with opportunities for creative and innovative learning interventions. We ended with a case that shows that consultants may be asked to help the organization address pervasive problems that affect operations and management practices.

In all, both here and throughout this book, we aimed to provide both breadth and depth concerning the learning consultant's potential roles in designing and implementing learning interventions. We showed the value consultants bring to clients and specifically how psychological research and practice complement the design and delivery of learning experiences. We also showed how interventions can add value to the individual learner, teams, and the organization. Learning takes place in a broad context, and consultants are well positioned to provide value to clients and learners.

RECOMMENDED READINGS

Barbazette, J. (2006). *Training needs assessment: Methods, tools, and techniques.* San Francisco, CA: Pfeiffer.

Biech, E. (Ed.). (2014). *ASTD handbook: The definitive reference for training and development* (2nd ed.). Alexandria, VA: ASTD Press.

Carliner, S. (2015). *Training design basics.* Alexandria, VA: ASTD Press.

DeChurch, L. A., & Marks, M. A. (2006). Leadership in multiteam systems. *Journal of Applied Psychology, 91,* 311–329. http://dx.doi.org/10.1037/0021-9010.91.2.311

Durlach, P. J., & Lesgold, A. M. (Eds.). (2012). *Adaptive technologies for training and education.* New York, NY: Cambridge University Press.

Kapp, K. M. (2010). *Learning in 3D: Adding a new dimension to enterprise learning and collaboration.* New York, NY: Pfeiffer.

Noe, R. A. (2015). *Employee training and development.* New York, NY: McGraw-Hill.

Stolovitch, H. D., & Keeps, E. J. (2011). *Telling ain't training.* Alexandria, VA: ASTD Press.

References

Aguinis, H., & Kraiger, K. (2009). Benefits of training and development for individuals and teams, organizations, and society. *Annual Review of Psychology, 60,* 451–474. http://dx.doi.org/10.1146/annurev.psych.60.110707.163505

American Psychological Association (2007). Guidelines for education and training at the doctoral and postdoctoral levels in consulting psychology/organizational consulting psychology. *American Psychologist, 62,* 980–992. http://dx.doi.org/10.1037/0003-066X.62.9.980

Anderson, C. (2016). Learning delivery—E-learning and mobile gaining ground. *Chief Learning Officer, 15*(8), 50–52. http://www.clomedia.com/2016/08/17/learning-delivery-e-learning-and-mobile-gaining-ground/

Anderson, M. C., Bjork, R. A., & Bjork, E. L. (1994). Remembering can cause forgetting: Retrieval dynamics in long-term memory. *Journal of Experimental Psychology: Learning, Memory, and Cognition, 20,* 1063–1087. http://dx.doi.org/10.1037/0278-7393.20.5.1063

Asencio, R., & DeChurch, L. A. (2017). Assessing collaboration within and between teams: A multiteam systems perspective. In A. A. von Davier, Z. Mengxiao, & P. C. Kyllonen (Eds.), *Innovative assessment of collaboration: Methodology of educational measurement and assessment* (pp. 37–50). Cham, Switzerland: Springer. http://dx.doi.org/10.1007/978-3-319-33261-1_3

ASTD Research. (2014). *Playing to win: Gamification and serious games in organizational learning.* Alexandria, VA: Author. Retrieved from https://www.td.org/Publications/Research-Reports/2014/Playing-to-Win

Bakker, A. B., Demerouti, E., & Sanz-Vergel, A. I. (2014). Burnout and work engagement: The JD–R approach. *Annual Review of Organizational Psychology and Organizational Behavior, 1,* 389–411. http://dx.doi.org/10.1146/annurev-orgpsych-031413-091235

Bandura, A. (2001). Social cognitive theory: An agentic perspective. *Annual Review of Psychology, 52*, 1–26. http://dx.doi.org/10.1146/annurev.psych.52.1.1

Bartlett, F. C. (1932). *Remembering: A study in experimental and social psychology.* Cambridge, England: Cambridge University Press.

Bedwell, W. L., Weaver, S. J., Salas, E., & Tindall, M. (2011). Emerging conceptualizations of adult training and learning. In M. London (Ed.), *The Oxford handbook of lifelong learning* (pp. 450–471). New York, NY: Oxford University Press. http://dx.doi.org/10.1093/oxfordhb/9780195390483.013.0143

Bell, B. S., & Kozlowski, S. W. J. (2002). Adaptive guidance: Enhancing self-regulation, knowledge, and performance in technology-based training. *Personnel Psychology, 55*, 267–306. http://dx.doi.org/10.1111/j.1744-6570. 2002.tb00111.x

Bell, B. S., & Kozlowski, S. W. J. (2010). Toward a theory of learner-centered training design: An integrative framework of active learning. In S. Kozlowski & E. Salas (Eds.), *Learning, training, and development in organization* (pp. 263–300). New York, NY: Routledge. http://psycnet.apa.org/record/2008-13469-008

Bell, B. S., Tannenbaum, S. I., Ford, J. K., Noe, R. A., & Kraiger, K. (2017). 100 years of training and development research: What we know and where we should go. *Journal of Applied Psychology, 102*, 305–323. http://dx.doi.org/ 10.1037/apl0000142

Bertua, C., Anderson, N., & Salgado, J. F. (2005). The predictive validity of cognitive ability tests: A UK meta-analysis. *Journal of Occupational and Organizational Psychology, 78*, 387–409. http://dx.doi.org/10.1348/096317905X26994

Biech, E. (Ed.). (2014). *ASTD handbook: The definitive reference for training and development* (2nd ed.). Alexandria, VA: Association for Talent Development.

Biesta, G., & Tedder, M. (2007). Agency and learning in the lifecourse: Towards an ecological perspective. *Studies in the Education of Adults, 39*, 132–149. http://dx.doi.org/10.1080/02660830.2007.11661545

Bjork, R. A. (1970). Positive forgetting: The noninterference items intentionally forgotten. *Journal of Verbal Learning and Verbal Behavior, 9*, 255–268. http:// dx.doi.org/10.1016/S0022-5371(70)80059-7

Block, P. (2011). *Flawless consulting: A guide to getting your expertise used* (3rd ed.). San Francisco, CA: Jossey-Bass/Wiley.

Borana, J. (2016). Applications of artificial intelligence and associated technologies. *Proceeding of International Conference on Emerging Technologies in Engineering, Biomedical, Management and Science* [ETEBMS-2016], 5–6 March, 2016. Retrieved from https://www.scribd.com/document/338142051/ETEBMS-2016-ENG-EE7

Bowman, J., & Wilson, J. P. (2008). Different roles, different perspectives: Perceptions about the purpose of training needs analysis. *Industrial and Commercial Training, 40*, 38–41. http://dx.doi.org/10.1108/00197850810841639

Cannon, T. (2016). *Exploratory case study of the Department of Navy's talent management system* (Doctoral dissertation). Retrieved from ProQuest Dissertations. (No. 10196589)

Capelli, P. (1999). *The new deal at work: Managing the market-based employment relationship.* Boston, MA: Harvard Business School Press.

Chen, G., & Klimoski, R. J. (2007). Training and development of human resources as work: Is the state of our science strong? *Human Resource Management Review, 17*, 180–190. http://www.sciencedirect.com/science/journal/10534822/17/2

Cotton, D. (2016). *The smart solution book: 68 Tools for brainstorming, problem solving and decision making.* Harlow, England: Pearson.

Crick, D. R., & Yu, G. (2008). Assessing learning dispositions: Is the *Effective lifelong learning inventory* valid and reliable as a measurement tool? *Educational Research, 50*, 387–402. http://dx.doi.org/10.1080/00131880802499886

CrossKnowledge (2016). Do you need an annual learning report? (and how to build it). *Chief Learning Officer, 15*, 34–35.

Danziger, K. (2008). *Marking the mind: A history of memory.* Cambridge, England: Cambridge University Press. http://dx.doi.org/10.1017/CBO9780511810626

DeChurch, L. A., & Marks, M. A. (2006). Leadership in multiteam systems. *Journal of Applied Psychology, 91*, 311–329. http://dx.doi.org/10.1037/0021-9010.91.2.311

Diamante, T. (2009). Authentic performance: The valuation of behavior as a negotiated business outcome. In J. Smither & M. London (Eds.), *Performance management: Putting research into action* (pp. 491–526). New York, NY: John Wiley & Sons.

Diamante, T. (2011). Leadership development programs that work: Individual transformation by design. In M. London (Ed.), *The Oxford handbook of lifelong learning.* New York, NY: Oxford University Press. http://dx.doi.org/10.1093/oxfordhb/9780195390483.013.0055

Diamante, T., & London, M. (2002). Expansive leadership in the age of digital technology. *Journal of Management Development, 21*, 404–416. http://dx.doi.org/10.1108/02621710210430597

Diamante, T., & Primavera, L. (2004). The professional practice of executive coaching.: Principles, practices and decisions. *International Journal of Decision Ethics, 1*, 85–114.

Dweck, C. S. (1986). Motivational processes affecting learning. *American Consultant, 41*, 1040–1048. http://dx.doi.org/10.1037/0003-066X.41.10.1040

Eddy, E. R., Tannenbaum, S. I., Lorenzet, S. J., & Smith-Jentsch, K. A. (2005). The influence of a continuous learning environment on peer mentoring behaviors. *Journal of Managerial Issues, 17*, 383–395. http://www.jstor.org/stable/40604508

Executive Office of the President. (2016). *Artificial intelligence, automation, and the economy.* Washington, DC: White House. Retrieved from https://obamawhitehouse.archives.gov/sites/whitehouse.gov/files/documents/Artificial-Intelligence-Automation-Economy.PDF

Fahy, P. J. (2008). Characteristics of interactive online learning. In T. Anderson (Ed.), *The theory and practice of online learning* (2nd ed., pp. 167–199). Edmonton, Alberta, Canada: AU Press. Retrieved from http://biblioteca.ucv.cl/site/colecciones/manuales_u/99Z_Anderson_2008-Theory_and_Practice_of_Online_Learning.pdf

FEDCAP Solution Series: Business in the 21st Century. (2016). *The intersection of workforce and economic development: Why it matters to employers* [Proceedings of panel discussion]. New York, NY: FEDCAP. Retrieved from http://www.fedcap.org/solutionseries-intersection-of-workforce-and-economic-development

Ferrazzi, K. (2014). Getting virtual teams right. *Harvard Business Review, 92*, 120–123. Retrieved from https://hbr.org/2014/12/getting-virtual-teams-right

Fiore, S. M., Wiltshire, T. J., Oglesby, J. M., O'Keefe, W. S., & Salas, E. (2014). Complex collaborative problem-solving processes in mission control. *Aviation, Space, and Environmental Medicine, 85*, 456–461. http://dx.doi.org/10.3357/ASEM.3819.2014

Frese, M., Gielnik, M. M., & Mensmann, M. (2016). Psychological training for entrepreneurs to take action: Contributing to poverty reduction in developing countries. *Current Directions in Psychological Science, 25*, 196–202. http://dx.doi.org/10.1177/0963721416636957

Frey, C. B., & Osborne, M. A. (2017). The future of employment: How susceptible are jobs to computerization? *Technological Forecasting and Social Change, 114*, 254–280. http://dx.doi.org/10.1016/j.techfore.2016.08.019

Gale, S. F. (2016). BBVA Bancomer plays the change game. *Chief Learning Officer, 15*, 44–49. https://www.researchgate.net/profile/Alfonso_Bustos/publication/297020031_BBVA_Bancomer_Plays_the_Change_Game/links/56dc8fd908aebabdb41425b4/BBVA-Bancomer-Plays-the-Change-Game.pdf

Glaub, M., & Frese, M. (2011). A critical review of the effects of entrepreneurship training in developing countries. *Enterprise Development & Microfinance, 22*, 335–353. http://dx.doi.org/10.3362/1755-1986.2011.035

Goldsmith, M., Lyons, L. S., & McArthur, S. (Eds.). (2012). *Coaching for leadership: Writings on leadership from the world's greatest coaches* (3rd ed.). San Francisco, CA: Pfeiffer.

Goodstone, M., & Diamante, T. (1998). Organizational use of therapeutic change: Strengthening multisource feedback systems through interdisciplinary coaching. *Consulting Psychology Journal: Practice and Research, 50,* 152–163. http://dx.doi.org/10.1037/1061-4087.50.3.152

Grant, H., & Dweck, C. S. (2003). Clarifying achievement goals and their impact. *Journal of Personality and Social Psychology, 85,* 541–553. http://dx.doi.org/10.1037/0022-3514.85.3.541

Gregory, J. B., & Levy, P. E. (2015). *Using feedback in organizational consulting.* Washington, DC: American Psychological Association. http://dx.doi.org/10.1037/14619-000

Greenwald, T. (2017, March 10). How AI is transforming the workplace. *The Wall Street Journal.* Retrieved from https://www.wsj.com/articles/how-ai-is-transforming-the-workplace-1489371060

Hackman, J. R. (2001). *Leading teams: Setting the stage for great performances.* Boston, MA: Harvard Business School Press.

Hardt, O., Nader, K., & Nadel, L. (2013). Decay happens: The role of active forgetting in memory. *Trends in Cognitive Sciences, 17,* 111–120. http://dx.doi.org/10.1016/j.tics.2013.01.001

Hattori, S. (2016). *The McKinsey edge: Successful principles from the world's most powerful consulting firm.* New York, NY: McGraw-Hill Education.

Hogan, J., Barrett, P., & Hogan, R. (2007). Personality measurement, faking, and employment selection. *Journal of Applied Psychology, 92,* 1270–1285. http://dx.doi.org/10.1037/0021-9010.92.5.1270

Jeanneret, R., & Silzer, R. (Eds.). (1998). *Individual psychological assessment: Predicting behavior in organizational settings.* San Francisco, CA: Jossey-Bass.

Judge, R. T., Erez, A., Bono, J. E., & Thoresen, C. J. (2003). The core self-evaluations scales: Development of a measure. *Personnel Psychology, 56,* 303–331. http://dx.doi.org/10.1111/j.1744-6570.2003.tb00152.x

Kaminski, K., & Lopes, T. (2009). *Return on investment: Training and development.* Alexandria, VA: Society for Human Resource Management.

Kanfer, R., & Ackerman, P. L. (1989). Motivation and cognitive abilities: An integrative/aptitude–treatment interaction approach to skill acquisition [Monograph]. *Journal of Applied Psychology, 74,* 657–690. http://dx.doi.org/10.1037/0021-9010.74.4.657

Kapp, K. M. (2010). *Learning in 3D: Adding a new dimension to enterprise learning and collaboration.* New York, NY: Pfeiffer.

Kapp, K. (2016a). Playing games leads to better learning. *Chief Learning Officer*, *15*, 50–53. Retrieved from http://cedma-europe.org/newsletter%20articles/ Clomedia/Playing%20Games%20Leads%20to%20Better%20Learning%20 (Jul%2016).pdf

Kapp, K. M. (2016b). Reflections on games and gamification for learning [Blog post]. Retrieved from http://karlkapp.com/2016-reflections-on-games-and-gamification-for-learning/

Keller, P. A., & Keller, P. (2010). *Six sigma demystified* (2nd ed.). New York, NY: McGraw-Hill Education.

Kelly, K. (2013). *Got game? The use of gaming in learning and development.* Chapel Hill: University of North Carolina Kenan-Flagler Business School. Retrieved from http://www.kenan-flagler.unc.edu/~/media/Files/documents/ executive-development/UNC-Got-Game-Final.pdf.

Kilmann, R. H. (1994). Managing ego energy for personal and organizational success. Adapted from R. H. Kilmann, I. Kilmann, & Associates. *Managing ego energy: The transformation of personal meaning into organizational success.* San Francisco, CA: Jossey-Bass. Retrieved from http://www.kilmanndiagnostics. com/managing-ego-energy-personal-and-organizational-success

Kirkpatrick, D. L. (1994). *Evaluating training programs: The four levels.* San Francisco, CA: Berrett-Koehler.

Kirkpatrick, D. L., & Kirkpatrick, J. D. (2006). *Evaluating training programs: The four levels* (3rd ed.). San Francisco, CA: Berrett-Koehler.

Knowles, M. (1975). *Self-directed learning.* Chicago, IL: Follett.

Knowles, M. (1984). *Andragogy in action.* San Francisco, CA: Jossey-Bass.

Kolb, D. A. (1976). Management and the learning process. *California Management Review*, *18*, 21–31. http://dx.doi.org/10.2307/41164649

Kolb, D. A. (1981). Learning styles and disciplinary differences. In A. W. Chickering (Ed.), *The Modern American College.* San Francisco, CA: Jossey-Bass.

Kolb, D. A. (2015). *Experiential learning: Experiences as the source of learning and development* (2nd ed.). Upper Saddle River, NJ: Pearson Education.

Kolb, D. A., Osland, J., & Rubin, I. (1995a). *Organizational behavior: An experiential approach to human behavior in organizations* (6th ed.). Englewood Cliffs, NJ: Prentice Hall.

Kolb, D. A., Osland, J., & Rubin, I. (1995b). *The organizational behavior reader* (6th ed.). Englewood Cliffs, NJ: Prentice Hall.

Kozlowski, S. W. J., & Salas, E. (Eds.). (2012). *Learning, training, and development in organizations.* New York, NY: Routledge.

Kraiger, K. (2008). Transforming our models of learning and development: Web-based instruction as enabler of third-generation instruction. *Industrial and*

Organizational Psychology: Perspectives on Science and Practice, 1, 454–467. http://dx.doi.org/10.1111/j.1754-9434.2008.00086.x

Kraiger, K. (2014). Looking back and looking forward: Trends in training and development research. *Human Resource Development Quarterly*, 25, 401–408. http://dx.doi.org/10.1002/hrdq.21203

Kraiger, K., & Wolfson, N. (2011). Assessing learning needs and outcomes in lifelong learning support systems. In M. London (Ed.), *The Oxford handbook of lifelong learning* (pp. 441–449). New York, NY: Oxford University Press. http://dx.doi.org/10.1093/oxfordhb/9780195390483.013.0140

Lacerenza, C. N., & Salas, E. (2014). Improving collaboration: Guidelines for team training. *Journal of Translational Medicine & Epidemiology*, 2, 1–10. Retrieved from https://www.jscimedcentral.com/TranslationalMedicine/translationalmedicine-spid-collaboration-science-translational-medicine-1028.pdf

Lacerenza, C. N., Zajac, S., Savage, N., & Salas, E. (2014). Team training for global virtual teams: Strategies for success. In J. L. Wildman & R. L. Griffith (Eds.), *Leading global teams: Translating multidisciplinary science to practice* (pp. 91–121). New York, NY: Springer.

Li, J. (2016). Technology advancement and the future of HRD research. *Human Resource Development International*, 19, 189–191. http://dx.doi.org/10.1080/13678868.2016.1181846

Locke, A. E., & Latham, G. (2013). *New developments in goal setting and task performance.* New York, NY: Routledge.

Lombardo, M. M., & Eichinger, R. W. (2000). *The career architect development planner* (3rd ed.). Minneapolis, MN: Lominger Limited.

London, M. (1996). Redeployment and continuous learning in the 21st century: Hard lessons and positive examples from the downsizing era. *The Academy of Management Executive*, 10, 67–79. http://www.jstor.org/stable/4165354

London, M. (Ed.). (2011). *The Oxford handbook of lifelong learning.* New York, NY: Oxford University Press.

London, M., & Diamante, T. (2002). Technology-focused expansive professionals: Developing continuous learning in the high-technology sector. *Human Resource Development Review*, 1, 500–524. http://dx.doi.org/10.1177/1534484302238438

London, M., & Hall, M. J. (2011). Unlocking the value of Web 2.0 technologies for training and development: The shift from instructor-controlled, adaptive learning to learner-driven generative learning. *Human Resource Management*, 50, 757–775. http://dx.doi.org/10.1002/hrm.20455

London, M., & Sessa, V. I. (2006). Continuous learning in organizations: A living systems analysis of individual, group, and organization learning.

In F. J. Yammarino, & F. Dansereau (Eds.), *Research in Multi-Level Issues: Vol. 5. Multi-level issues in social systems* (pp. 123–172). Bingley, England: Emerald Group.

London, M., & Sessa, V. I. (2007). How groups learn, continuously. *Human Resource Management, 46,* 651–669. http://dx.doi.org/10.1002/hrm.20186

Lowe, K. (2016, July 20). Diagnosing and coaching teams: The 3 essential and 3 enabling conditions of team effectiveness (Part 1 of 2) [Blog post]. Retrieved from http://www.teamcoachingzone.com/diagnosing-coaching-teams-3-essential-3-enabling-conditions-team-effectiveness-part-1-2/

Lowman, R. L. (Ed.). (2002). *Handbook of organizational consulting psychology: A comprehensive guide to theory, skills, and techniques.* San Francisco, CA: Jossey-Bass.

Lowman, R. L. (2016). *An introduction to consulting psychology: Working with individuals, groups, and organizations.* Washington, DC: American Psychological Association. http://dx.doi.org/10.1037/14853-000

Lowman, R. L., & Cooper, S. E. (2018). *The ethical practice of consulting psychology.* Washington, DC: American Psychological Association. http://dx.doi.org/10.1037/0000058-000

Lundvall, B. A., & Johnson, B. (1994). The learning economy. *Journal of Industry Studies, 1,* 23–42. http://dx.doi.org/10.1080/13662719400000002

Marks, M. A., Zaccaro, S. J., & Mathieu, J. E. (2000). Performance implications of leader briefings and team-interaction training for team adaptation to novel environments. *Journal of Applied Psychology, 85,* 971–986. http://dx.doi.org/10.1037/0021-9010.85.6.971

Marquardt, M. (2011). *Optimizing the power of action learning: Real-time strategies for developing leaders, building teams and transforming organizations* (2nd ed.). Boston, MA: Nicholas Brealey.

Marsick, V. J., & Watkins, K. E. (1990). *Informal and incidental learning in the workplace.* London, England: Routledge.

Marsick, V. J., & Watkins, K. E. (2001). Informal and incidental learning. In S. B. Merriam (Ed.), *The new update on adult learning theory* (pp. 25–34). San Francisco, CA: Jossey-Bass.

Marsick, V. J., Nicolaides, A., & Watkins, K. E. (2014). Adult learning theory and application in HRD. In N. E. Chalofsky, T. S. Rocco, & M. L. Morris (Eds.), *Handbook of human resource development* (pp. 40–61). New York, NY: John Wiley & Sons.

Martinelli, R. J., & Milosevic, D. Z. (2016). *Project management toolbox: Tools and techniques for the practicing project manager.* New York, NY: John Wiley & Sons.

Mathieu, J. E., Tannenbaum, S. I., & Salas, E. (1992). Influences of individual and situational characteristics on measures of training effectiveness.

Academy of Management Journal, 35, 828–847. http://dx.doi.org/10.2307/256317

Maurer, T. J., Weiss, E. M., & Barbeite, F. G. (2003). A model of involvement in work-related learning and development activity: The effects of individual, situational, motivational, and age variables. *Journal of Applied Psychology, 88*, 707–724. http://dx.doi.org/10.1037/0021-9010.88.4.707

Mayer, R. E. (2001). *Multimedia learning.* New York, NY: Cambridge University Press.

McAdams, D. P., & Pals, J. L. (2006). A new big five: Fundamental principles for an integrative science of personality. *American Psychologist, 61*, 204–217. http://dx.doi.org/10.1037/0003-066X.61.3.204

McCauley, C. D., & McCall, M. W., Jr. (Eds.). (2014). *Using experience to develop leadership talent.* San Francisco, CA: Jossey-Bass. http://dx.doi.org/10.1002/9781118829417

McCrae, R. R., & John, O. P. (1992). An introduction to the five-factor model and its applications. *Journal of Personality, 60*, 175–215. http://dx.doi.org/10.1111/j.1467-6494.1992.tb00970.x

Meyers, M. C., & van Woerkom, M. (2014). The influence of underlying philosophies on talent management: Theory, implications for practice, and research agenda. *Journal of World Business, 49*, 192–203. http://dx.doi.org/10.1016/j.jwb.2013.11.003

Mezirow, J. (2000). *Learning as transformation: Critical perspectives on a theory in progress.* San Francisco, CA: Jossey-Bass.

Mone, E., & London, M. (2010). *Employee engagement through effective performance management: A practical guide for managers.* New York, NY: Routledge.

Moon, M. J., & Lee, L. H. (2017). *Introducing a new talent management system for Korea's public officials*, KDI School of Public Policy & Management (Paper No. 17-03). http://dx.doi.org/10.2139/ssrn.2970878

Morgan, R. E., & Berthon, P. (2008). Market orientation, generative learning, innovation strategy and business performance inter-relationships in bioscience firms. *Journal of Management Studies, 45*, 1329–1353. http://dx.doi.org/10.1111/j.1467-6486.2008.00778.x

Morrison, C. (2016). *The gamification of organizational learning.* New York, NY: American Management Association. http://www.amanet.org/training/articles/printversion/The-Gamification-of-Organizational-Learning.aspx

Naim, M. F., & Lenka, U. (2017). Talent management: A burgeoning strategic focus in Indian IT industry. *Industrial and Commercial Training, 49*, 183–188. http://dx.doi.org/10.1108/ICT-12-2016-0084

Natale, S., & Diamante, T. (2005). Five stages of executive coaching: Better process makes better practice. *Journal of Business Ethics, 59*, 361–374. http://dx.doi.org/10.1007/s10551-005-0382-2

National Research Council. (2000). *How people learn: Brain, mind, experience, and school: Expanded edition.* Washington, DC: National Academies Press. http://dx.doi.org/10.17226/9853

New Leadership Learning Center. (2013). *Leadership development program: Curriculum and trainers' guide.* Baltimore, MD: New Leadership Learning Center.

Osborn, C. (2016). What do employees think about their training? *Training, 53,* 120–123. Retrieved from https://trainingmag.com/trgmag-article/what-do-employees-think-about-their-training

Pashler, H., McDaniel, M., Rohrer, D., & Bjork, R. (2009). Learning styles: Concepts and evidence. *Psychological Science in the Public Interest, 9,* 105–119. http://dx.doi.org/10.1111/j.1539-6053.2009.01038.x

Paterson, K. (2009). *Desperately seeking solutions.* Markham, Ontario, Canada: Pembroke.

Phillips, J. J., & Phillips, P. P. (2016). *Handbook of training evaluation and measurement methods.* New York, NY: Routledge.

Pyzdek, T., & Keller, P. (2014). *The six sigma handbook* (4th ed.). New York, NY: McGraw-Hill.

Rabin, R. (2015). *Blended learning for leadership: The CCL approach* [White Paper]. Greensboro, NC: Center for Creative Leadership. Retrieved from http://www.ccl.org/wp-content/uploads/2015/04/BlendedLearningLeadership.pdf

Revans, R. W. (2011). *ABC of action learning.* Burlington, VT: Gower.

Roth, M. (2011). *TRADOC-sponsored simulation wins Serious Games Challenge* [Press release]. Retrieved from http://www.army.mil/article/70550/

Russell, L. (2015). *Leadership training.* Alexandria, VA: Association for Talent Development.

Salas, E., & Cannon-Bowers, J. A. (2001). The science of training: A decade of progress. *Annual Review of Psychology, 52,* 471–499. http://dx.doi.org/10.1146/annurev.psych.52.1.471

Salas, E., Tannenbaum, S. I., Kraiger, K., & Smith-Jentsch, K. A. (2012). The science of training and development in organizations: What matters in practice. *Psychological Science in the Public Interest, 13,* 74–101. http://dx.doi.org/10.1177/1529100612436661

Schein, E. H. (2016). *Humble consulting: How to provide real help faster.* Oakland, CA: Berrett-Koehler.

Schmidt, A. M., & Ford, J. K. (2003). Learning within a learner control training environment: The interactive effects of goal orientation and metacognitive instruction on learning outcomes. *Personnel Psychology, 56,* 405–429. http://dx.doi.org/10.1111/j.1744-6570.2003.tb00156.x

Senge, P. M., Kleiner, A., Roberts, C., Ross, R. B., & Smith, B. J. (2014). *The fifth discipline fieldbook: Strategies and tools for building a learning organization.* New York, NY: Crown Business.

Sessa, V. I., & London, M. (2006). *Continuous learning in Organizations: Individual, group, and organizational perspectives.* Mahwah, NJ: Erlbaum.

Silberstang, J., & Diamante, T. (2008). Phases and targeted interventions: Improving team learning and performance. In V. Sessa & M. London (Eds.), *Work group learning: Understanding, improving and assessing how groups learn in organizations* (pp. 347–364). New York, NY: Lawrence Erlbaum Associates.

Silberstang, J., & London, M. (2009). How groups learn: The role of communication patterns, cue recognition, context facility, and cultural intelligence. *Human Resource Development Review, 8,* 327–349. http://dx.doi.org/10.1177/1534484309337300

Simpson, M. (2014). *Unlocking potential: Seven coaching skills that transform individuals, teams, and organizations.* Grand Haven, MI: Grand Harbor Press.

Sitzmann, T., Bell, B. S., Kraiger, K., & Kanar, A. M. (2009). A multilevel analysis of the effect of prompting self-regulation in technology-delivered instruction. *Personnel Psychology, 62,* 697–734. http://dx.doi.org/10.1111/j.1744-6570.2009.01155.x

Sonesh, S. C., Coultas, C. W., Lacerena, C. N., Marlow, S. L., Benishek, L. E., & Salas, E. (2015). The power of coaching: A meta-analytic investigation. *Coaching: An International Journal of Theory, Research and Practice, 8,* 73–95. http://dx.doi.org/10.1080/17521882.2015.1071418

Tannenbaum, S. (1997). Enhancing continuous learning: Diagnostic findings from multiple companies. *Human Resource Management, 36,* 437–452. http://dx.doi.org/10.1002/(SICI)1099-050X(199724)36:4<437::AID-HRM7>3.0.CO;2-W

Tannous, J. (2016, December). *Program development at the intersection of mission, market, and money.* Educational Advisory Board presentation, State University of New York at Stony Brook.

Taylor, P. J., Russ-Eft, D. F., & Chan, D. W. L. (2005). A meta-analytic review of behavior modeling training. *Journal of Applied Psychology, 90,* 692–709. http://dx.doi.org/10.1037/0021-9010.90.4.692

Thomson, L. (2016). *Your guide + workbook to developing employees into leaders* [ebook]. Retrieved from https://learning.linkedin.com/content/dam/me/learning/EMW/lil-guide-developing-employees-into-leaders.pdf

Thornton, G. C., III, & Gibbons, A. M. (2009). Validity of assessment centers for personnel selection. *Human Resource Management Review, 19,* 169–187. http://dx.doi.org/10.1016/j.hrmr.2009.02.002

Toth, T. A. (2015). *Technology for trainers* (2nd ed.). Alexandria, VA: ATD Press.

Truong, H. M. (2016). Integrating learning styles and adaptive e-learning system: Current developments, problems and opportunities. *Computers in Human Behavior, 55*(Part B), 1185–1193. http://dx.doi.org/10.1016/j.chb.2015.02.014

Ulrich, D., Kerr, S., & Ashkenas, R. (2002). *The GE workout: How to implement GE's revolutionary method for busting bureaucracy and attacking organizational problems—fast!* New York, NY: McGraw-Hill.

Van Velsor, E., McCauley, C. D., & Ruderman, M. N. (Eds.). (2010). *The Center for Creative Leadership handbook of leadership development* (3rd ed.). San Francisco, CA: Jossey-Bass.

Vygotsky, L. (1978). *Mind in society: The development of higher psychological processes.* Cambridge, MA: Harvard University Press.

Wageman, R., Hackman, J. R., & Lehman, E. (2005). Team diagnostic survey: Development of an instrument. *The Journal of Applied Behavioral Science, 41,* 373–398. http://dx.doi.org/10.1177/0021886305281984

Wilson, E. (2016). 5 Tech leaders step up learning and development to engage employees in training [Blog post]. Retrieved from https://trainingmag.com/5-tech-leaders-step-learning-and-development-engage-employees

Wittrock, M. C. (1992). Generative learning processes of the brain. *Educational Psychologist, 27,* 531–541. http://dx.doi.org/10.1207/s15326985ep2704_8

Yao, M. (2017). *Conversational interfaces: Principles of successful bots, chatbots, messaging apps, and voice experiences.* New York, NY: Topbots.

Zichermann, G., & Cunningham, C. (2011). *Gamification by design: Implementing game mechanics in web and mobile apps.* Sebastopol, CA: O'Reilly Media.

Index

About the Authors

Manuel London, PhD, is dean of the College of Business and Distinguished Professor of Management at the Stony Brook University, where he has taught and been an administrator for the past 28 years. His PhD is in industrial–organizational psychology from The Ohio State University. Starting his career on the organizational behavior faculty at the University of Illinois, Champaign–Urbana, he subsequently was a researcher and human resources practitioner at AT&T for 12 years. As a practitioner and consultant, Dr. London has worked on program development in the areas of training, leadership development, performance management, and group learning. His books include *The Power of Feedback: Giving, Seeking, and Using Feedback for Performance Improvement* (3rd ed., 2015), and *Continuous Learning: Directions for Individual and Organization Development* (with Valerie Sessa, 2006). He is the editor of *The Oxford Handbook of Lifelong Learning* (2011) and *Performance Management: Putting Research Into Practice* (with James W. Smither, 2009).

Thomas Diamante, PhD, is president, Division of Organizations, Consulting & Work for the New York State Psychological Association. As executive vice president and practice director at CCA, Inc., a human capital consultancy, he consults for C-level, cross-cultural, cross-industry executives to enhance individual and organizational performance. He advises venture capital firms on nonfinancial due diligence to reduce investment risk and provides executive coaching for the Fortune 500. Dr. Diamante's highly diverse client portfolio reflects global financial services, media, world-renowned cultural institutions, global consumer products, technology start-ups, as well as federal agencies and municipalities. Human resources consultations include management education, selection, performance management and succession planning, and leadership development. His PhD is in industrial–organizational psychology from The Graduate Center, City University of New York; he is a New York State–licensed psychologist. Dr. Diamante's industrial–organizational background is complemented by clinical training in behavior change management from The Institute for Behavior Therapy in New York. He is formerly of Merrill Lynch (Global Securities Research & Economics), where he held the position of vice president of corporate strategy and organization development; KPMG Consulting (BearingPoint), where he served as senior manager and lead change consultant; and Altria, where he started his career as national manager, human resources and executive development. He is Board Chair, Emeritus for enACT, Inc., an educational nonprofit serving New York City schoolchildren and is the author of *Effective Interviewing and Information Gathering: Proven Tactics to Improve Your Questioning Skills* (2013).